The CONSTITUTION *in* EXILE

How the Federal Government Has
Seized Power by Rewriting the
Supreme Law of the Land

This book is dedicated to
PRESIDENT THOMAS JEFFERSON,
who authored
The Declaration of Independence,
and who,
alone among the presidents,
allowed tyrannical laws to expire,
and who reminded posterity that
"When the people fear the government, there is tyranny.
When the government fears the people, there is liberty."

ALSO BY ANDREW P. NAPOLITANO:

Constitutional Chaos:
What Happens When the Government
Breaks Its Own Laws
(Thomas Nelson, Inc. 2004)

CONTENTS

PREFACE

Do we still have a Constitution?

Before you jump to answer too quickly, hear me out. Today the federal government recognizes no limitations on its power. It has utterly rejected the idea, integral to the Constitution, that it is one of limited powers, carefully and precisely delegated. Today the federal government does whatever it wants to do. In essence, the feds say: "Don't like the drinking age in South Dakota? Well, just threaten their highway funds and they'll come around. Is the FBI frustrated by public scrutiny? Just make it a felony *to speak* about receiving certain self-written search warrants. Don't like the idea of kids working after school? Just make shipment of the furniture they make illegal. Think any of this might be unconstitutional? Well, we'll just let the courts sort it out."

It may sound harsh, but I have heard similar thoughts expressed time and again. They reveal an utter contempt for the Constitution, a mind-set that believes that when it comes to government, bigger is better, and a nanny state attitude that says the bureaucrats and fat cats in Washington D.C. know better what enhances our freedom than we do.

And Congress is not the only culprit. Two of our most historically revered presidents committed crimes that today are unthinkable.

Abraham Lincoln and Franklin Delano Roosevelt simply ignored the Constitution's basic restraints on the government. Lincoln arrested thousands of folks because *they disagreed with him,* and FDR arrested over one hundred thousand Americans because of *their race and ethnicity.*

How did we get here? How did thirteen idealistic colonies, founded under the rubric of freedom and individualism, not security and Big Government, allow an out-of-control, monster federal government to regulate the most intimate aspects of our lives?

The purpose of this book is to tell the unhappy story of liberty lost, federalism trampled, and Big Government run amok. The United States Constitution established the framework for a federal government holding only specific, enumerated powers. Yet the federal government has actually involved itself or threatened to do so in a vast array of human behavior, nowhere even hinted at in the Constitution. Today the federal government intrudes itself into the blood alcohol level of automobile drivers, the legal drinking age for alcohol, the amount of wheat a farmer can grown for his own use, the ability of a terminally ill cancer patient to grow medical marijuana for personal use, the amount of sugar manufacturers can use in ketchup, rebuilding private homes after hurricanes, regulating steroids in athletes' blood, regulating the size of toilets in private homes, preventing states from enhancing the freedom of their citizens to join publicly funded groups, using the concept of federalism when it suits the Congress but rejecting it when Congress disagrees, saving banks from the thieves who robbed them, regulating state court systems, and forcing states to increase penalties for state crimes.

The Founders gave us a small, discrete federal government, one of strictly limited powers; powers to address issues that are federal in nature. The Congress has confused *federal* with *national,* and has chosen to regulate any issue that it thinks affects more than one state, irrespective of the absence of federal power and the true presence of state power.

This book addresses how and why our central government went so far astray and what we should do to correct it. Almost as if by design, every generation in the federal government, from George Washington to George W. Bush, has only sought more power for itself. They have ignored the constitutional limits on their powers and, in essence, sent the Constitution into exile.

How did they do it? How have they gotten away with it? What will become of our freedoms if the Constitution is exiled?

Introduction

ROOTS OF THE CURRENT DEBATE

What Rosa Parks Knew That We Forget

To understand the Constitution and where it came from, we must look at its counterpart, the Declaration of Independence, and we must understand the Natural Law that grounds both documents.

Whether they realize it or not, most contemporary legal scholars and politicians in the Western world stand behind two competing theories about the origins of law and liberty: Natural Law and Positivism. The Natural Law school of thought argues that freedom comes by virtue of being created human, from our very nature, and holds that laws created by kings or legislatures are always secondary to the Natural Law. It is the royal flush against which any other law is merely a pair of deuces.

This is not a new concept. The Greek writer Sophocles "recognizes the reality that human laws are subject to a higher law," according to my professor of constitutional law and jurisprudence at Notre Dame Law School, Charles E. Rice. Similarly, Aristotle observed that "one part of what is politically just is natural, and the other part is legal." Cicero described it as "the highest reason, implanted in Nature, which commands what ought to be done and forbids the opposite." Writes Cicero, "Right is based, not upon men's opinion [from popular legislatures], but upon Nature."

In more recent times, Justice Clarence Thomas, writing about the "higher law political philosophy" of the Founding Fathers, stated, "Natural rights and higher law arguments are the best defense of liberty and of limited government. Moreover, without recourse to higher law, we abandon our best defense of judicial review—a judiciary active in defending the Constitution. Rather than being a justification for the worst type of judicial activism, higher law is [the] only alternative to the willfulness of both run-amok majorities [in Congress] and run-amok judges [in federal courts]."[1]

Natural Law theory teaches that the law extends from human nature, which is created by God. The Natural Law theory states that because all human beings desire freedom from artificial restraint and because all human beings yearn to be free, our freedoms must stem from our very humanity—and ultimately from the Creator of humanity.

Perhaps no one can answer the question of "What is the Natural Law?" more clearly than Professor Rice: "Natural law will seem mysterious if we forget that everything has a law built into its nature. . . . If you eat a barbed-wired sandwich, it will not be good for you. If you want your body to function well, you ought not to treat it as if it were a trash compactor. Natural law is easy to understand when we are talking about physical nature. But it applies as well to the moral sphere."

Think of your human experience as derived from God, as Rice has suggested, like a car that is derived from its manufacturer. God (or the Universal Spirit if you are not religious) is the manufacturer of your life. God created you and sent along a manual, much like the vehicle manufacturer includes in the glove compartment of your car (does anyone actually keep gloves in them?). The manufacturer wants you to drive your car successfully so that you and your friends will buy more cars, so it gives you tips on how to maintain the car and how to get out of trouble should it break down. Likewise, according to the Natural Law, God has equipped you with a manual—some say it is the Bible, others the Tanakh, others the Koran, others a rational mind. No matter what you believe, the Natural Law of the world can be seen running throughout any of the time-tested documents of Western Civilization. "It would be a strange motorist who would resent the existence of that manual and refuse to look at it," says Rice.[2]

Strange indeed when you think of the important, real-world implications and consequences of Natural Law. Take the case of Rosa Parks.

Parks's famous refusal to give up her seat on a bus in 1955 in Alabama was a demonstration of "a proper reading of the Natural Law," according to Rice, because she refused to obey an unjust law. She played the royal flush and trumped the segregationists, who relied on the prejudiced opinion of popular majorities, not higher law.

Said Martin Luther King Jr., "A just law is a man-made code that squares with the moral law or the law of God. . . . An unjust law is a code that is out of harmony with the moral law. To put it in the terms of Saint Thomas Aquinas, 'unjust law is a human law that is not rooted in eternal law and natural law.'"

These concepts about law and liberty played an important role in the American experience from the very start.

NATURAL RIGHTS

The language of the Declaration of Independence refers specifically to God-given rights, those received by virtue of our humanity. The very first sentence claims a God-given right to be separate and equal beings—existing apart from a political power. The Declaration says that it is possible and even sometimes necessary—like Parks's refusal writ large—for "one people to dissolve the political bonds which have connected them with another, and to assume . . . the separate and equal station to which the laws of nature and of nature's God entitle them. . . ." God grants "certain unalienable rights." Government is supposed to secure them.

If the text of the Declaration is not sufficient evidence of the role of Natural Law in the formation of our country as an independent state, Thomas Jefferson's studies and writings reveal a strong adherence to Natural Law principles. Jefferson was heavily influenced by the writings of John Locke and Thomas Paine. He borrowed considerably from the language and philosophies of both men in drafting the Declaration. For example, both Locke and Paine used the word "unalienable" to describe human rights.

Locke, in his *Second Treatise on Government*, wrote, "Reason . . . teaches all Mankind . . . that being all equal and independent, no one ought to harm another in his Life, Health, Liberty, or Possessions." That immunity from harm includes harm caused by government—language and thoughts clearly echoed in the Declaration and its understanding of natural rights.

In *The Rights of Man*, Paine wrote that these natural rights include "all the intellectual rights, or rights of the mind, and also all those rights of acting as an individual for his own comfort and happiness, which are not injurious to the natural rights of others." The government, Jefferson and Paine argued, is necessary to secure those rights in the civil context.[3]

Jefferson's own writings, prior to and after the Declaration, also display his belief in Natural Law. In a legal argument written in 1770, Jefferson wrote that "Under the law of nature, all men are born free, every one comes into the world with a right to his own person, which includes the liberty of moving and using it at his own will. This is what is called personal liberty, and is given him by the Author of nature, because necessary for his own sustenance." Note that Jefferson chose to capitalize the *A* in *Author*—a reference to God that would have been crystal-clear to his contemporaries. Jefferson could be more explicit when he needed to be. "The God who gave us life, gave us liberty at the same time," he declared in July 1774.[4]

It is clear from the text of the Declaration, and the influences and writings of its principal drafter, that Natural Law principles establish the rights referenced in the Declaration of Independence. And that is precisely how constitutional originalists such as Justice Clarence Thomas interpret it.

The significance of the Declaration for constitutional scholars is that it is believed to contain the philosophical underpinnings of the Constitution. In other words, an understanding of Natural Law, its conferral of rights upon men and women, and the relationship between those rights and the role of government is fundamental to understand and interpret the Constitution properly.

WHY SHOULD WE CARE?

That freedom comes not from government, not from the consent of the governed, not from the community, but from God and is inherent to our humanity has profound effects on modern jurisprudence. It means that our basic freedoms—such as freedom of the press, freedom of speech, freedom of religion, freedom of association, freedom to travel, and freedom from arbitrary restraints—cannot be taken away by the government unless we are convicted of violating Natural Law, and the government can only convict us if it follows what is called "procedural due process."

Due process means that we know in advance of the violations of Natural Law that the government will prosecute, that we are fully notified by the government of the charges against us, that we have a fair trial with counsel before a truly neutral judge and jury, that we can confront and challenge the government's evidence against us, that we can summon persons and evidence on our own behalf, that the government must prove our misdeeds beyond a reasonable doubt, and that we have the right to appeal the outcome of that trial to another neutral judge.

Under the Natural Law, the only way that any of our natural rights can be taken away is by conviction by a jury. Our rights cannot be legislated away, no matter how universally accepted the legislation, and they cannot be commanded away, no matter how beloved, benign, or correct the commander may be.

Because free speech is a natural right and can only be taken away after due process, it cannot be taken away simply because a legislature says so. Thus, Natural Law protects minority rights from incursion by the majority. Neither Congress nor any state legislatures can declare that freedom of speech no longer exists, or take any words—which are only expressions of ideas—and make them illegal.

Under Natural Law, if Congress made it unlawful to speak out against abortion, or if a state governor issued a decree that ordered Christians and Jews to cease worshiping, judges would surely invalidate those acts even if there were no First Amendment protecting freedom of speech and religion because the right to speak and worship as we wish comes from our humanity, not from the government or from the First Amendment. Because of that, judges can enforce those rights—regardless of the misguided will of Congress or a state governor.

In this same way, Natural Law also prevents the majority from having its way all of the time. For example, voters cannot directly (through a referendum) or indirectly (through a legislature) take property that properly belongs to *A* and give that property to *B. Why not?* Because under Natural Law, that legislation would exceed the power of any government by violating the right of *A* to the use and enjoyment of his own property. Property owners have the right to use and enjoy what is theirs whether or not the positive (i.e., written down) law protects those rights.

The Founders certainly saw things this way. Constitutional limits on government, as Alexander Hamilton once said, "serve to protect the security of Property . . . against the majority's will." Soon after the states ratified the Bill of Rights, Supreme Court Justice Samuel Chase wrote, "An act of the Legislature (for I cannot call it a law) contrary to the great first principles of the social compact, [i.e., the Natural Law] cannot be considered a rightful exercise of legislative authority. . . ."

Under Natural Law, legislatures have unwritten limitations imposed upon them, and those limitations prevent a legislature, no matter how one-sided the vote and no matter how popular the legislation, from enacting a law which interferes with a natural right. Congress could take a lesson from Rice's theory that "The Natural Law provides a guide through which we can safely and rightly choose to love God by acting in accord with our nature and by helping others to do the same. We can know the requirements of Natural Law through reason unaided by explicit revelation."[5] Natural Law declares that when the people created state legislatures, and when the states created the Congress, they never gave these bodies the authority to interfere with natural rights. They did not do so because they could not do so. As we observed earlier, no one can take away another's natural rights except a jury, following due process.

Natural Law also commands certain prohibitions. For example, since enslaving a person or taking an innocent life is always wrong,

Natural Law commands that slavery and murder are unlawful, whether the legislature declares them so or not.

Natural Law does, however, recognize that not all rights are natural, and some rights do come from the state. For example, the right to drive a motor vehicle on a government-owned roadway is a right that comes from the state; hence, the government can lawfully regulate it (e.g., by requiring a driver's license, limiting speed, etc.) and lawfully take it away (e.g., from habitual drunk drivers).

THE NEGATIVE OF POSITIVE

Positivist theory is more or less the opposite of Natural Law theory. Under Positivism, the law is whatever those in power say it is, whether that decision is democratic or dictatorial in nature. Positivism demands that all laws be written down, and requires that there are no theoretical or artificial restraints (such as Natural Law) on the ability of the government to enact whatever laws it wishes. No higher law exists; deuces beat a royal flush if enough people in power say so.

In this theory the majority always rules and always gets its way, since there are no minority rights to be protected—except whatever rights the majority might condescend to grant.

To follow our earlier example, if, under a Positivist system, a state legislature or the Congress were to enact legislation prohibiting public criticism of abortion, or a state governor ordered Christians and Jews to cease worshiping, so long as the legislature was legally elected and it followed its own rules in enacting the legislation, and so long as the legislation proscribed criticism of abortion or authorized the governor's behavior, the prohibition of speech and the interference with the free exercise of religion would be the law of the land, and no court could interfere with it.

In the Positivist scheme, rights come from government, and

government can always repeal what it grants. Critics of Positivism have argued that it leads to the tyranny of the majority. These critics remind us that Hitler and the Nazis were popularly elected. Once in power, under a Positivist legal theory, they passed all sorts of horrific laws, all of which were "lawfully" enacted. The Nazis rejected Natural Law, which protects the minority, and we all know what happened to the minority in Hitler's Germany.

In America, the Declaration of Independence is traditionally referred to as the sheet anchor of our liberties. It does not grant liberties; it publicly pronounces and secures them, just as an anchor secures a boat. Similarly, the Constitution of the United States also does not grant rights, but rather recognizes their existence, guarantees their exercise, and requires the government to protect them.

Just look at the First Amendment to the Constitution: "Congress shall make no law respecting an establishment of religion or prohibiting the free exercise thereof; or abridging the freedom of speech. . . ." This clearly reveals that the authors of the amendment—the Founders—recognized that freedom of religious worship and freedom of speech preexisted, and thus come from some source other than, the Constitution. Properly understood then, the First Amendment is not a grant of rights to the people, but a restriction on government that prevents it from infringing on the rights the people already have. It also implies that not only may Congress *not* interfere with freedom of speech or the free exercise of religion, but Congress *must prevent* all who act in the name of the government from interfering with them as well.

IN A LAND OF NO CONSTRAINTS

Throughout this book I will be discussing rights and liberties. As I will use the terms, rights are specific freedoms specifically guaranteed by the Constitution, such as freedom of speech, freedom of the press, and the right to bear arms; liberties are more general freedoms, like the right to travel, the right to think whatever you please, and the right to be left alone, with which the government may not interfere without due process.

As the reader can no doubt safely guess by now, I am a strong and fervent believer in Natural Law. The only valid laws are those grounded in a pursuit of goodness. Anything else—like taking property from *A* and giving it to *B*, like silencing an unpopular minority, like interfering with freedom of worship—is an unjust law and, theoretically, need not be obeyed, just like the law that told Rosa Parks to find her seat in the rear of the bus. No government may enact laws interfering with our natural freedoms, no matter how popular the enactment.

The Positivist would say that since the majority in a free society gives freedom, the majority can take it away. Natural Law says only God gives freedom, and the government can only take it away as a punishment for violating Natural Law, and then only through due process.

To a Positivist, the government's goal is to bring about the greatest benefit to the greatest number of people.

Under Natural Law, the only legitimate goal of government is to secure liberty, which is the freedom to obey one's own free will and conscience, rather than the free wills or consciences of others, no matter whether those others are in the streets, in City Hall, in the state legislatures, on Capitol Hill, or in the White House.

The problem today in America—the greatest and gravest threat to personal freedom in this country—is that the Positivists are carrying the day. Under their sway, the government violates the law while busily passing more legislation to abridge our liberties. The government recognizes no constraints on its power and enacts whatever laws it wishes.

If we wish to survive the near future with our rights intact, we need to understand the size and scope of the threat. We must also understand its true identity: *a government that claims it can give you rights can also take them away.*

Throughout the coming pages, we will explore the gravity and disaster inherent in that simple fact. First we'll look at the nature of the Constitution—what it says and what it means. Then, chapter by chapter, we'll explore how politicians and judges have slowly driven the Constitution and its restraints on the government into exile.

1

THE LAW OF THE LAND

What the Constitution Really Says

After the Boston Tea Party, in which American colonists disguised as Mohawk Indians dumped a fortune of tea into Boston Harbor in protest of British economic policies, Parliament passed a series of heavy-handed laws to punish the colonies for their insubordinate attitude. The laws, dubbed the "Intolerable Acts" by the colonists, closed the port of Boston to trade, made public meetings illegal, and barred Massachusetts courts from exercising jurisdiction over British soldiers.[1]

In response, the Continental Congress met for the first time in September 1774 in Philadelphia. Twelve of the original thirteen colonies sent delegates. Out of the bunch (Maryland, Delaware, Connecticut, New Jersey, New Hampshire, Massachusetts, New York, Pennsylvania, North Carolina, Virginia, Rhode Island, and South Carolina), only Georgia was not represented. After an unsuccessful attempt to smooth things over by petition to King George, it met again in 1775. By this time colonists were already fighting scattered battles against British soldiers. The Revolutionary War had unofficially begun.

It was clear by early 1776 that independence was the only option for the American colonists. In June 1776, the Continental Congress met in Philadelphia to write a document declaring independence. The result, the Declaration of Independence, was primarily penned by Thomas Jefferson and approved by the Continental Congress on July 3, 1776.

But independence was not enough to see them through the times ahead. The meeting in June 1776 had another purpose as well: to draft, as John Adams wrote, "the form of a Confederation to be entered into between these Colonies."

The American colonies had formed a union, but this union's only responsibility was to protect the independence of the colonies from the British. While each colony (now known as a "state") was free and independent, it was unclear just what the relationships and duties of the states would be to each other. Representatives from each state signed the Declaration of Independence, but the states were acting independently when they sent representatives to do this. The states were sovereign entities that the Continental Congress could not directly control. Essentially, there was no binding central national government.

Given their experience under British rule, the states were understandably reluctant to submit to any form of central authority. The document known as the Articles of Confederation was the first effort to set forth the nature and extent of the confederated relationship among the several states. It took longer to approve the Articles of Confederation than it had taken to adopt the Declaration of Independence. The Congress did not agree to conditions of the Articles of Confederation until November 1777, and the document was not formally ratified until 1781. When Maryland, the last state to approve, signed the document, "a firm league of friendship" was formed, and the Congress of the Confederation came into existence.

The loose group of states was now known as "the United States of America." The states were in complete control of all their affairs except for the powers specifically given by them to Congress under the Articles. "Each state retains its sovereignty, freedom, and independence, and every power, jurisdiction, and right, which is not expressly delegated to the United States," stated Article II. This language is similar (save for the word "expressly") to the principle of the Tenth Amendment of the U.S. Constitution.

The three branches of government as we know them today had still not been created. Under the Articles, Congress could create committees and appoint people to serve as necessary for managing the government. However, a large, centralized bureaucracy was out of the question. A president was elected by the Electoral College, which consisted of members of Congress, but he was limited to a one-year term and could only run once every three years. The president presided over a committee made up of one representative from each state. Congress controlled the president and his committee, and the president did not have much power by today's standards.

The new national government had few functions and little power. A national system of courts was not established. Congress could not tax the people of the United States. *(Ah, the good old days!)* It could ask the states for tax money, but this "as a practical matter, amounted to little more than a request for voluntary donations to the national treasury." Likewise, it could "coin money," but it never printed any. Entering into treaties with foreign nations and maintaining an army were solely the role of Congress, but for the most part the states maintained the real power under the Articles. The states could individually issue money, which some did recklessly. Each state could regulate trade, even if its laws contradicted the laws of other states. Congress could not effectively regulate trade, collect taxes, or rule on the validity of laws. Changes to this system of government were difficult because they required unanimous consent among the states, which meant that one state could hamstring the entire nation. Most historians believe that "this system quickly crippled the new nation's economic strength and proved untenable."[2]

One of the most problematic things at this time was the fact that Congress could not regulate the movement of goods between merchants across state borders. When Virginia and Maryland allowed only ships registered in their respective states to trade in Virginia and Maryland, Congress could do nothing more than suggest other options. Several states, including New York, Pennsylvania, and South Carolina, "taxed and irritated the adjoining States trading through them."[3] The commercial conflicts among the states would soon become ruinous.

BACK TO THE DRAWING BOARD

By 1787, Congress realized that it needed to resolve the commercial problems caused by the Articles of Confederation. The Constitutional Convention of 1787 was held in Philadelphia to amend the articles. But instead of proposing amendments which would have required unanimous consent, a new Constitution was drafted, which would become effective once it was ratified by only nine states.

When the convention started, the delegates recognized that all the states shared two common goals:

1. To form a representational democracy, which is a republican form of government.
2. To create a limited central government, which is a government with express written powers and limitations.

The problem was that, while the delegates may have shared these goals, they represented different areas of the United States with different beliefs concerning centralized government. In other words, they were on the same page, but had different ideas about what they were reading.

The delegates were eventually able to compromise on most issues. The debates were particularly heated between free and slave states, large and small states, and Northern and Southern states. In order to minimize their differing opinions, the delegates conducted their meetings behind closed doors. We have, of course, detailed notes of what was said, but *the first great debate over American values—perhaps the most significant in all our history—excluded the public and the press.*

Most of the delegates were or would become notable figures in American history. George Washington was the chairman of the convention. Alexander Hamilton, James Madison, and Benjamin Franklin actively participated throughout the convention.

The debates continued for over four months. The delegates finally reached the "Great Compromise" under which a new national government with three branches, legislative, executive, and judicial, was formed. The legislative branch would consist of a House of Representatives representing the people and a Senate representing the states as sovereign entities. Each state would have an equal number of representatives in the Senate, but representation in the House of Representatives would be based on population.

SEPARATING THE POWERS

Madison believed that a large, centralized government would become tyrannical. "The accumulation of all powers, legislative, executive, and judiciary, in the same hands, whether of one, a few, or many, and whether hereditary, self appointed, or elective, may justly be pronounced the very definition of tyranny," Madison wrote in *Federalist* 47. One way to limit this threat was to separate powers and divide the duties of government, so that one branch becomes a check on the power and encroachment of the others.

While each branch of the government must check the power of the others, Madison did not think that they must be completely separate. He wrote that the branches could interact "unless these departments be so far connected and blended as to give to each a constitutional control over the others. . . ."[4] However, Madison believed that each branch of the government should only exercise those powers granted to it under the Constitution.

Under the new Constitution, the executive branch was to include a president and vice president. The president would serve a term of four years. He would be the commander in chief of the armed forces and have the power to appoint a variety of officials, including justices to a newly created Supreme Court. An electoral college would elect the president, and the citizens would elect the members of the electoral college.

Relatively few specific powers were given to the judicial branch. The Supreme Court would be the highest court of the United States, and it could exercise both original and appellate jurisdiction, depending on the case.

Delegates from each state approved the Constitution, although some were disturbed that a Bill of Rights had not been included. In July 1789, the Constitution became *the supreme law of the land of the United States of America.*

The U.S. Constitution is now the oldest continuously effective written constitution in the world. Before it was drafted, a system of checks and balances was unheard of in any country. Through vision, hard work, fear of recent history, perseverance, and fidelity to the principles of Natural Law, the delegates were able to create a successful written Constitution that would stand the test of time.

But that's not entirely correct, is it?

THE SLAVERY COMPROMISES

Not every part of the new Constitution was consistent with Natural Law. Even though the states had been able to agree on a Constitution, there were still unresolved issues. There were at least five hundred thousand slaves in the United States at this time. Even my hero of the era, Thomas Jefferson, owned more than one hundred.[5]

Slavery had been an issue during the Constitutional Convention. Regrettably, the issue was political, not moral. Because representation in the House of Representatives was based on population, states in the South would gain an advantage if slaves were included when calculating their population. Northern states adamantly opposed this since the slaves were denied virtually every liberty recognized by the Constitution; they were not citizens and, obviously, could not vote. Hypocritically, the "rulers" of the Southern states wanted their slaves to "count" where it helped them, but not to count when it really mattered—i.e., in terms of humanity and liberty. The compromise reached was that each slave would be counted as three-fifths of a free person when determining population. Both sides were able to agree to this unfortunate "three-fifths compromise."

Fugitive slaves who escaped to free states were also a point of contention. Regarding this debate, Madison wrote in *Federalist* 54, "We must deny the fact, that slaves are considered merely as property, and in no respect whatever as persons. The true state of the case is, that they partake of both these qualities: being considered by our laws, in some respects, as persons, and in other respects as property." *Ouch!*

Southern states were concerned that fugitive slaves would not be returned. Northern states wanted to see the slaves freed. In another unfortunate compromise that was necessary to assure agreement among the states, the Constitution provided that fugitive slaves were to be returned to their "owners." This was horrific.

CHECKS, BALANCES, AND POWER GRABS

The Constitution established a system of checks and balances to distribute power. The executive, legislative, and judicial branches can all exercise certain powers over the other branches. This system is designed to avoid tyranny by one branch over the other and thus over the people.

For example, under the Constitution the president can veto congressional legislation. Congress can override the president's veto, but only by a two-thirds vote of each house, then pass legislation into law. The judicial branch can subsequently declare the law unconstitutional and void. Members of the judicial branch are appointed by the president and confirmed by the Senate. If judges act improperly, then Congress can impeach them and remove them from office. But these checks and balances have not always worked as planned.

Ever since the Civil War, Congress has usurped powers that the Constitution left to the states, often with the approval of the executive and judicial branches. Congress has not hesitated to apply its powers broadly under the Commerce Clause. This clause gives Congress the power "to regulate commerce with foreign nations, and among the several states, and with the Indian tribes." When the Constitution was written, interstate commerce was minimal. Today, nearly every manufactured good, or one of its components, travels across a state line at some point. The simple act of a component crossing a state line from one merchant to another is the constitutional basis Congress claims to impose limitless regulations on the conditions of manufacture and use of the product of which the component becomes a part.

By defining interstate commerce so broadly, Congress has claimed the power to regulate almost anything. During the past century, Congress has regulated, among other things, homegrown agricultural and medicinal products, pornography, violence, and illegal guns simply by calling them all "commerce." Occasionally, the Supreme Court will strike down a law and limit the extent of Congress's regulatory power. Since the presidency of Franklin D. Roosevelt, however, this has been rare.

By regulating everything from wheat to water, Congress has infringed on the rights of the states and individuals. Even activities taking place entirely on private property or inside someone's home have not escaped congressional regulation. Where the executive and judicial branches have failed to check and balance these congressional power grabs, new spheres of federal power have been created, and state and individual rights have been unjustifiably and unconstitutionally curtailed. This is a direct assault on the individual liberties that our tripartite federal government was designed to prevent.

BUYING OFF FEDERALISM

In addition to the three branches of the central government, the Founders also envisioned strong state governments that would both supplement federal regulations and serve as a check on them. Powers not delegated to the federal government were retained by the states. This system, known as federalism, preserves the autonomy of the states and, as a consequence, contains the spread of federal power—a pressing concern of the Founders following the colonial period.

In recent times, however, Congress has intruded upon areas that had been left to the states for two hundred years. There is, for instance, no federal police power in the Constitution. The "police power" is the right and obligation of the states to legislate for the health, safety, welfare, and morality of persons present in the states. But now federal agents can arrest people for crimes related to drugs, the environment, car theft, domestic violence, and other things that Congress considers to have an aggregate effect on interstate commerce. This intrudes upon the police power that the Constitution has left entirely to the states.

Roads and other infrastructure were solely state issues until the 1950s. But Congress now regulates interstate highways, waterways, and other channels of interstate commerce with little regard for the states. Money for the construction of highways has been used to influence states to conform to the will of Congress. This was seen in the 1980s when Congress demanded a nationwide drinking age of twenty-one and threatened any state that did not conform with a reduction in its allotment of federal highway money. After bitter litigation, the states complied. More recently, Congress pulled the same trick to force all states to adopt a uniform blood alcohol content standard for prosecuting drunk drivers. Where does Congress get the power to regulate the amount of alcohol in a person's blood?

All the states have far less combined power than Congress because of its ability to control federal spending. Indeed, because of the power of the federal purse strings, states have been coerced into sacrificing some of their sovereign powers. Congress now influences state government to a far greater extent than the Founders ever imagined.

EIGHTEEN POWERS

In establishing our system of separate powers, checks and balances, and federalism, the Founders limited Congress—and thus the will of the Positivists—to eighteen specific, enumerated, and delegated powers. Those three words are important. *Specific* means something that is definite or explicitly set forth. *Enumerated* refers to things that are listed individually by their identifying characteristics. *Delegated* refers to a power that has been assigned by one party to another.

The Founders did this to create a system of government in which power is diffused between the states and the central government and diffused further within the central government. State sovereignty is maintained; and because governmental power was not to be concentrated anywhere, individual liberty is protected. When it usurps powers left to the people or the states or even the other two branches of the federal government, Congress attacks structures intended to diffuse power and maintain individual freedom.

Let us now examine briefly the eighteen (*that's all there are)* specific, enumerated, delegated powers which the Constitution has given to Congress.

Limited Power 1. "The Congress shall have Power To lay and collect Taxes, Duties, Imposts and Excises, to pay the Debts and provide for the common Defense and general Welfare of the United States; but all Duties, Imposts and Excises shall be uniform throughout the United States."

In this section, the Constitution gives Congress power to impose taxes and spend taxpayers' money for the "general welfare." The power to tax is very broad, but the judicial branch has limited this power in certain cases. As the Sixteenth Amendment declares, Congress may impose a tax on personal income; but it could not do so until that amendment was adopted because the Constitution, prior to that amendment, prohibited direct taxes on persons by Congress.

It is unclear from the text exactly what is meant by "general welfare." It is understood to be a qualification on the power of Congress to tax, not a separate grant of power. Therefore, Congress may not regulate for the general welfare, but it may tax and spend for the general welfare. Under a do-gooder, busybody, Big Government view of the General Welfare Clause, Congress can undertake any action as long as it is for the general welfare. This is an abuse of the enumerated powers granted to Congress. Under a freedom-loving, Big Government-fearing view of the General Welfare Clause, Congress can only spend for the general welfare when it has permission to do so under another enumerated power. This limits what Congress can do in the name of the "general welfare" by requiring that expenditures of federal tax dollars be such that *all* persons can enjoy them.

Building bridges confronts the general welfare dispute directly. Fans of Big Government argue that as long as the public can use the bridge, it exists for the general welfare, including the now infamous "bridge to nowhere" in Alaska that joins a town of forty-five people to a nearby city at a cost of $223 million of your federal tax dollars (that's just the minimum; Taxpayers for Common Sense figure the final taxpayer payout at $315 million). They would also argue that any federal giveaway is for the general welfare because it at least temporarily alleviates the suffering of the recipients. Fans of limited government argue that if the Founders wanted Congress to have the power to build bridges, they would have said so in the Constitution. As we shall see later, when the Supreme Court addressed this dispute, it compromised.

Here's another contemporary example. After Hurricane Katrina destroyed most of New Orleans in September 2005, President George W. Bush proposed legislation that would have the American taxpayer rebuild public roads and private property. Since a rebuilt road could theoretically be used by the general public, one could argue that its construction was for the general welfare. Since rebuilding someone's house, however, is not even arguably for the "general welfare"—rather for the specific welfare of the specific recipient of the taxpayers' money—this cannot constitutionally be done. But Congress will do it nevertheless.

Limited Power 2. "To borrow Money on the credit of the United States; Congress may borrow money by issuing bonds or by other means." Once Congress has borrowed money, the federal government has a binding obligation to repay the debt. This is, unfortunately, the basis for the government's power to borrow at our children's expense, mortgage away their future, and amass enormous national debt that future generations will have to bear as a result of governmental excesses. Without this constitutionally permitted credit card, we might actually see moderate and restrained spending in Washington, since the government, absent the power to borrow, would have to balance its budgets or find itself out of business. Instead, the federal government can spend what it doesn't have and leave the tab for "the second shift." And most of Washington seems to agree with Vice President Dick Cheney that "Deficits don't matter." I do not.

Limited Power 3. "To regulate Commerce with foreign Nations, and among the several States, and with the Indian Tribes." Under a broad socialist reading of "commerce" and what affects it, Congress claims it can regulate virtually anything, and, as we will see in detail, it has done so. Jefferson argued that "regulate" simply means "to make regular," that is, to keep the states and others from interfering with the regular movement of goods between merchants across interstate borders. As discussed later, Congress has hardly adhered to this view.

Limited Power 4. "To establish a uniform Rule of Naturalization, and uniform Laws on the subject of Bankruptcies throughout the

United States." Congress alone can define the process by which immigrants from foreign countries become American citizens.

Limited Power 5. "To coin Money, regulate the Value thereof, and of foreign Coin, and fix the Standard of Weights and Measures." This power appears self-explanatory, but it must be considered along with *Limited Power 6.*

Limited Power 6. "To provide for the Punishment of counterfeiting the Securities and current Coin of the United States." Congress has claimed that this power and *Limited Power 5* allow it to charter federal banks and use them to regulate the economy. I don't know about you, but I don't see those powers being specifically enumerated and delegated to Congress in the Constitution. Maybe I'm just not good at reading between the lines.

Limited Power 7. "To establish Post Offices and post Roads." Congress has used this power to enact legislation criminalizing competition with the post office for First-Class mail, thus effectively forcing us to use FedEx or UPS. Who today trusts the post office with anything timely or important?

Limited Power 8. "To promote the Progress of Science and useful Arts, by securing for limited Times to Authors and Inventors the exclusive Right to their respective Writings and Discoveries." This allows Congress to pass copyright and patent laws.

Limited Power 9. "To constitute Tribunals inferior to the Supreme Court." The only court formally established under the enumerated powers is the U.S. Supreme Court. Congress has created a system of lower federal courts under this limited power.

Limited Power 10. "To define and punish Piracies and Felonies committed on the high Seas, and Offences against the Law of Nations." Congress can protect ships on the high seas; piracy was a far more pervasive problem then than it is today.

Limited Power 11. "To declare War, grant Letters of Marquee and Reprisal, and make Rules concerning Captures on Land and Water." This section allows Congress—and only Congress—to declare war or sanction military activities by American persons and ships.

Limited Powers 12–14. "To raise and support Armies, but no Appropriation of Money to that Use shall be for a longer Term than two Years" (12). "To provide and maintain a Navy" (13). "To make Rules for the Government and Regulation of the land and naval Forces" (14). Congress can regulate the military. But for so-called "strict constructionists" who believe the Constitution must be interpreted as it was intended by the Founders in 1789, I ask: If the Constitution gives the power to create an army and navy, from whence does Congress have the power to create an air force? Is the air force unconstitutional? How about the coast guard?

Limited Power 15. "To provide for calling forth the Militia to execute the Laws of the Union, suppress Insurrections and repel Invasions." This gives Congress the power to federalize state militias, although several presidents have likewise ordered the militias into action and claimed they did not need the approval of Congress.

Limited Power 16. "To provide for organizing, arming, and disciplining, the Militia, and for governing such Part of them as may be employed in the Service of the United States, reserving to the States respectively, the Appointment of the Officers, and the Authority of training the Militia according to the discipline prescribed by Congress." Congress can ultimately regulate militias and the National Guard.

Limited Power 17. "To exercise exclusive Legislation in all Cases whatsoever, over such District (not exceeding ten Miles square) as may, by Cession of particular States, and the Acceptance of Congress, become the Seat of the Government of the United States, and to exercise like Authority over all Places purchased by the Consent of the Legislature of the State in which the Same shall be, for the Erection of Forts, Magazines, Arsenals, dock-Yards, and other needful Buildings." Congress is ultimately in charge of the District of Columbia, although it has delegated certain responsibilities to the local government. Congress is in charge of all forts, arsenals, and other military facilities owned by the federal government.

Limited Power 18. "To make all Laws which shall be necessary and proper for carrying into Execution the foregoing Powers, and all other Powers vested by this Constitution in the Government of the United States, or in any Department or Officer thereof." This is known as the "necessary and proper" power. It permits Congress to use only means that are *both* necessary *and* proper to carry out its powers. However, Congress has grossly misconstrued this clause. To Congress "necessary and proper" means anything helpful to further Congress's will.

It may be hard to believe, but the eighteen, specific, enumerated and delegated powers are the only powers the Constitution has granted to Congress. One of the focal points of this book is what Congress has done to expand and exploit those powers. It is clear from history and any cursory glance of current events that Congress has ignored its constitutional limits and has *given itself* a vast array of new powers.

WHY WE HAVE A BILL OF RIGHTS

Once the Constitution was written, some drafters presumed that it should be clear that the federal government was limited to the seventeen powers and one qualifier (the Necessary and Proper Clause) specified in the Constitution. Many of the drafters, however, were concerned about the potential for the federal government to expand its powers. In a letter to James Madison, Thomas Jefferson said that "a bill of rights is what the people are entitled to against every government on earth, general or particular; and what no just government should refuse. . . ."

The purpose of the Bill of Rights is to state in clear terms individual rights that cannot be impaired by Congress or the president. Yet the Founding Fathers—who considered freedom of speech, the right to bear arms, compensation for government seizures of private property, and freedom from unreasonable searches and seizures too important to be left unprotected by the Constitution—could not agree as how best to safeguard those rights.

Thomas Jefferson wrote, "I do not like . . . the omission of a bill of rights providing clearly . . . for freedom of religion, freedom of the press, protection against standing armies, restriction against monopolies, the eternal and unremitting force of the habeas corpus laws, and trials by jury. . . ." If he only could have anticipated the abuses and blatant disregard of those rights by modern-day local, state, and federal police. These gross abuses are the subject of many books, including my previous book, *Constitutional Chaos: What Happens When the Government Breaks Its Own Laws.*

Following John Locke and the Natural Law theorists, the Founding Fathers were most concerned about life, liberty, and personal property rights. The Bill of Rights was written to protect these rights from interference by the new government. The Founding Fathers were well aware of the atrocities committed by the monarchies of Europe, most notably the British crown. Prior to the American Revolution, they had been subjected to unreasonable searches, seizures of property without just compensation, and suppression of speech and other forms of political expression.

Not all of the Founding Fathers agreed with Jefferson's opinion that a Bill of Rights was necessary. Early drafts of the Bill of Rights indicate that there were originally twenty proposed amendments.

Eventually, twelve amendments were submitted to the states for approval, and only ten of these were ultimately approved. Some states did not agree with the principles of the amendments. Massachusetts, Connecticut, and Georgia did not formally approve the Bill of Rights until 1939.

The most notable omission from the early draft of the Bill of Rights is a list of "natural rights." The rights of life, liberty, the pursuit of happiness, and possessing property were not approved by the states and never became part of the present Bill of Rights, mainly due to opposition from slave-holding states and the debates that led to the three-fifths compromise.

Today, those who oppose natural rights argue that liberty and possessing property are not guaranteed by the Bill of Rights. But given all of the other protections that were passed into law, it is inconceivable that the Founding Fathers would have disregarded natural rights as unimportant, especially since most of these "self evident truths" are so eloquently set forth in the Declaration of Independence. Otherwise, there would have been no reason to guarantee a trial by jury, the assistance of counsel in criminal cases, and the Fifth Amendment prohibition against being forced to testify against oneself at a criminal trial.

An interesting effect of enacting a Bill of Rights was to strengthen the balance of powers. The judicial branch can enforce any rights that are firmly established in the Constitution or the amendments to it. The rights of individuals are best preserved when people can bring cases to court to enforce their rights. As Jefferson put it, "in the arguments in favor of a declaration of rights . . . one which has great weight with me [is] the legal check which it puts into the hands of the judiciary." Jefferson understood that individual liberties in the Bill of Rights could be effectively upheld by an independent judiciary.

Before the passage of the Bill of Rights, Jefferson said, "these restrictions, I think, are so guarded as to hinder evil only. However, if we do not have them [a recitation of natural rights] now, I have so much confidence in my countrymen as to be satisfied that we shall have them as soon as the degeneracy of our government shall render them necessary."

Jefferson believed strongly in the power of American judges to uphold the rights of individual citizens. One can only wonder what Jefferson would think of the state of individual liberties today.

INSIDE THE BILL OF RIGHTS

The Bill of Rights consists of ten amendments that, like the Constitution itself and the Declaration of Independence before it, are grounded by Natural Law. These ten amendments are designed to protect individual freedoms that the Founders considered natural rights, thus God-given, but feared that the new federal government might ignore. The Bill of Rights is supposed to prevent the federal government from denying these fundamental rights to any person. They reflect human nature in the absence of a tyrannical government.

Amendment 1. "Congress shall make no law respecting an establishment of religion, or prohibiting the free exercise thereof; or abridging the freedom of speech, or of the press; or the right of the people peaceably to assemble, and to petition the Government for a redress of grievances." Freedom of expression is part of human nature and cannot be in a truly free society denied absent due process.

Amendment 2. "A well regulated Militia, being necessary to the security of a free State, the right of the people to keep and bear Arms, shall not be infringed." This very necessary amendment is designed to keep the government in check and limit its power. It is necessary even today because, without firearms, how can people protect themselves from any oppressive tyrannical government?

Amendment 3. "No Soldier shall, in time of peace be quartered in any house, without the consent of the Owner, nor in time of war, but in a manner to be prescribed by law." This amendment addresses atrocities committed by British soldiers against the colonists before and during the American Revolution, and prohibits American soldiers from doing the same.

Amendment 4. "The right of the people to be secure in their persons, houses, papers, and effects, against unreasonable searches and seizures, shall not be violated, and no Warrants shall issue, but upon probable cause, supported by Oath or affirmation, and particularly describing the place to be searched, and the persons or things to be seized."

Supreme Court Justice Louis Brandeis once proclaimed that the chiefmost right is "the right to be le[f]t alone." In the present age, we call this the right to privacy. The Fourth Amendment was written to guarantee this right.

The Founders had personal experiences with British soldiers, the direct reaction to which led to this amendment. The British economy, like most of its European counterparts, was mercantilist. This meant that trade was heavily regulated for the maximum benefit of the mother country. To avoid all of the imposts and restrictions—which hampered business for colonial merchants and added heavy costs to goods for their customers—colonists resorted to a good deal of smuggling. How to stop the widespread practice? Parliament gave soldiers and officials nearly unlimited rights to search private buildings, including homes, for smuggled goods. Using self-written search warrants called Writs of Assistance, officials were able to demand entrance—even by force.

So the Fourth Amendment was crafted to protect privacy rights and to curtail unlimited search authority. Now only judges are allowed to issue search warrants and only where the circumstances are clearly laid out and limited. How else could an individual be truly free in a society if not by limiting the power of the government to prosecute only those persons as to whom there is real evidence of guilt? To the Founders, the thought of soldiers or government agents writing their own search warrants was anathema.

Amendment 5. "No person shall be held to answer for a capital, or otherwise infamous crime, unless on a presentment or indictment of a Grand Jury, except in cases arising in the land or naval forces, or in the Militia, when in actual service in time of War or public danger; nor shall any person be subject for the same offense to be twice put in jeopardy of life or limb; nor shall be compelled in any criminal case to be a witness against himself, nor be deprived of life, liberty, or property, without due process of law; nor shall private property be taken for public use, without just compensation."

The first section of this amendment provides the protection of a grand jury to people accused of a crime. Like trial juries, grand juries are composed of ordinary citizens. The purpose of a grand jury is to allow fellow citizens to determine whether the government can bring a criminal case against an accused person. To ensure a free and open society, citizens do not have to defend themselves from accusations by the government until they have been indicted by a grand jury of their peers. The protection of a grand jury does have certain limitations; military personnel do not have to be indicted by a grand jury during "time of war or public danger." This section is vague, and "cases arising in the land or naval forces" has been stretched to include enemy combatants or other people only tangentially connected to the military. But in essence, outside of military matters, a person must be formally indicted by a grand jury of his peers before having to defend himself for a serious federal crime.

The next section concerns double jeopardy. The Founders were concerned that persons would have to defend themselves against the government in repeated lengthy trials. This section of the amendment ensures that people will not have to go through a trial more than once for a particular charge. Mistrials, hung juries, and other procedural breakdowns may cause a defendant to undergo another trial, but once an acquittal has been granted or guilt has been determined, a person cannot be retried. Law enforcement officials have at times subverted this clause by retrying an acquitted state defendant on similar federal charges, and vice versa; courts have, unfortunately, allowed this.

The phrase that states a person shall not "be compelled in any criminal case to be a witness against himself" prevents a person from being forced to testify against himself, and it prohibits torture. The bigger idea here is to defend due process. A person being questioned by the police under duress may make a statement that incriminates himself to avoid abuse, whether or not the person committed the crime at issue or is perfectly innocent.

The next section of the Fifth Amendment is the Due Process Clause. It states that a person shall not "be deprived of life, liberty, or property"—a clear statement of a person's natural rights—"without due process of law." This means that the government must publicly and formally charge persons with a crime and prove their guilt beyond a reasonable doubt in a court of law. Due process has two key elements. One is the right to a fair prosecution (procedural due process); the other is a set of fundamental, natural rights that are understood in a free and orderly society (substantive due process).

The last section of the Fifth Amendment is known as the Takings Clause. The government cannot interfere with a person's natural right to own property without providing fair compensation for the taking. In order to seize private property for public use, the government must pay the owner a fair and reasonable price. The idea is to protect the right to own property, which is fundamental to a free and open society. What's more, a taking must only be for truly public use, like a road or bridge or school. Alexander Hamilton once said that "these two limitations serve to protect the security of property . . . against the majority's will." Unfortunately, the courts have failed to safeguard this right and have permitted governments to take private property against the will of the owner, then sell it to another private owner.

Amendment 6. "In all criminal prosecutions, the accused shall enjoy the right to a speedy and public trial, by an impartial jury of the State and district wherein the crime shall have been committed, which district shall have been previously ascertained by law, and to be informed of the nature and cause of the accusation; to be confronted with the witnesses against him; to have compulsory process for obtaining witnesses in his favor, and to have the Assistance of Counsel for his defense."

The Sixth Amendment provides many procedural safeguards to citizens accused of a crime. Defendants are entitled to a speedy jury trial. The jury will consist of the defendant's peers. Trials are to be public, and a defendant is entitled to confront all the witnesses against him; this means that a defendant can watch the testimony of hostile witnesses and cross-examine them to discredit their allegations.

One of the most important tenets of this amendment is the right to counsel. From the moment of arrest, a defendant is entitled to consult with a lawyer at any stage of the criminal trial process. He is entitled to have a lawyer present when he is questioned by the police and at his trial. This ensures that those with expertise in the law are present to monitor the government and make sure that it plays by the rules. Courts take violations of criminal procedure very seriously, and a serious infraction can result in the dismissal of all charges against even a guilty defendant. Better a guilty man go free than the rights of all citizens be thrown into jeopardy.

Defendants in criminal cases are also entitled to obtain witnesses to testify in their favor. A reluctant witness can be subpoenaed and forced by the court to say what he saw or knows, as long as the witness is not implicating himself in a crime. All of the provisions of the Sixth Amendment are designed to create a level playing field between criminal defendants and the government.

Amendment 7. "In Suits at common law, where the value in controversy shall exceed twenty dollars, the right of trial by jury shall be preserved, and no fact tried by a jury, shall be otherwise re-examined in any Court of the United States, than according to the rules of the common law." This guarantees jury trials in all civil suits in federal courts.

Amendment 8. "Excessive bail shall not be required, nor excessive fines imposed, nor cruel and unusual punishments inflicted." This amendment provides more protection to defendants in criminal cases and those who have been convicted of a crime.

Punishments cannot be excessive or exceptionally cruel. It is not completely clear what the Founders meant by "cruel," and some people have used this phrase to argue against the death penalty. However, the Founders were well aware of executions of convicted felons and made no provision to prevent this practice. More likely, the Eighth Amendment is designed to prevent torture of any person, whether or not they have been convicted of a crime, and punishment of any person in manner disproportionate to the harm caused by the crime or truly offensive to society's cultural norms.

Amendment 9. "The enumeration in the Constitution, of certain rights, shall not be construed to deny or disparage others retained by the people." Basically, the Founders set out to clarify that the language they used was not to be twisted in any manner to limit the rights of the people.

According to Professor Randy E. Barnett, "the Founders believed it was dangerous to enumerate any rights because the rights of the people are boundless. As James Wilson, a natural-rights theorist, explained, 'there are very few who understand the whole of these rights.'" Barnett has quite properly argued that all rights are not enumerable. No list could ever contain all the things to which free people are entitled. The sole boundary, according to Barnett, is that people's rights "are limited only by their imagination."[6]

Amendment 10. "The powers not delegated to the United States by the Constitution, nor prohibited by it to the States, are reserved to the States respectively, or to the people."

The Tenth Amendment makes it clear that the Constitution is a document of enumerated powers. If the Constitution does not give a power to the federal government, then it is left to the states and the people. Those in favor of Big Government claim that this amendment is just a "truism" and argue that the federal government can act broadly under the powers expressly granted to it. However, if the Founders had intended this result, then they would have reversed the wording of the Tenth Amendment and left all powers not specifically retained by the people to the federal government. *They did not.*

Here, the Founders explicitly affirmed the bedrock principles of federalism. If only John Marshall, Abraham Lincoln, Franklin Delano Roosevelt, George W. Bush, and every Congress had more regard for this amendment, as we shall see, America would be a very different—and much freer—place today.

2

THE RISE OF THE SUPREME COURT

John Marshall's Big Play

Today, the Supreme Court is a source of unending controversy: slim-margin decisions, contested rulings, scrutinized appointments, and threatened filibusters. The Supreme Court has incredible power and deals with some of the hottest issues confronting our society. That alone creates a volatile brew. But there's another element that really stokes the flaming controversies of our day: the Court is often called upon to apply the Constitution to subjects and disputes that the Founders could never have imagined: abortion, flag burning, or gay rights, for three quick examples.

Here is where the controversies usually center: Given that these are issues the Founders never dealt with, should the Court treat the Constitution as a living document, allowing judges to interpret it according to the times? Should the Court try to discern the Founders' "original intent" and apply it to these new situations and issues? Should the Court yield all deference to the rule of the majority in the legislature? Or . . . how about none of the above?

The Supreme Court serves an important function in the system of checks and balances. It is capable of overturning unconstitutional laws passed by the Congress and signed by the president, or enacted by the states, and it can stop the president from acting unconstitutionally. This makes the Court the last line of defense against the federal or state governments usurping powers that they are not permitted either because the Constitution does not allow it, or the Bill of Rights prohibits it, or Natural Law prevents it.

But how did we reach this point?

The judicial branch of the federal government should be a vigilant watchdog that rules on cases that come before it to protect our natural rights and to preserve the division of power established in the Constitution. The Founders intended the Court to serve as the interpreter of the law, although they did not spell it out in the Constitution. Because they failed to do so, at certain points in American history, we've had dramatic legal cases that have paved the way for the Supreme Court to take and exercise its role as the ultimate arbiter of the meaning of the Constitution. *Marbury v. Madison*, *Calder v. Bull*, and the poignant lesson in *Brown v. Board of Education* are particularly illustrative.

THE COURT'S STARRING ROLE

The presidential election of 1800 was drawing near and a great political battle was being fought. The two parties, the Democratic Republicans, also called the Anti-Federalists, and the Federalists, had differing visions of the direction in which the United States of America should go, with each side presenting differing views of the role of the federal government in the lives of individuals.

The Federalists, politically close to modern-day liberal Democrats and Big Government Republicans, had support in the Northeast and favored a broad reading of the Constitution in which a unified nation had a strong federal government at its helm. The

Democratic Republicans, closer to the modern-day conservative and libertarian Republicans, thought that the biggest threat to individual freedom was a tyrannical central government and that power in the hands of the common people and the states was preferred.[1] Both sides understood that control of the courts was crucial to the triumph of their ideas.

When the results of that close election of 1800 were in, Thomas Jefferson and the Anti-Federalists defeated John Adams and the Federalists. In fact, the Democratic Republicans won both the presidency and control of the Congress. But the Congress wouldn't change hands until the spring of 1801, and the courts were packed with Federalists who had been appointed by former President Washington and outgoing President Adams. Between the election and the inauguration, still several months away, the country was at a crossroads.

The problems started immediately. Jefferson beat Adams by a vote of seventy-three to sixty-five in the Electoral College, but the Electoral College voters did not distinguish their votes for president and vice president, so Jefferson and Aaron Burr, his running mate, both got seventy-three votes. The House of Representatives, still under Federalist control, had to break the tie—and thus decide the election. During the next six days, the votes were cast over thirty times but neither candidate received a majority. Finally, some Federalists, desiring an orderly transfer of power despite their open dislike of Jefferson, conceded and voted for the author of the Declaration of Independence. Jefferson's inauguration was held on March 4, 1801. The Twelfth Amendment, enacted in 1804, addressed the preceding conundrum by requiring electors to "name in their ballots the person voted for as president, and in distinct ballots the person voted for as vice president."

But the 1800 election and the following changing of the guard brought about an even more enduring conflict.

The Federalist-controlled Congress had enacted the Judiciary Act of 1789 which set up the nation's initial federal court system. In late February 1801, after it became apparent that the anti-Federalist Jefferson had defeated the Federalist Adams for the presidency, the Federalist-controlled Congress enacted legislation that created forty-two additional federal judgeships. On March 2, 1801, two days before he left office, Adams appointed forty-two Federalists to these courts. On March 3, the next day, the still Federalist-controlled Senate confirmed the judges.

William Marbury was one of these late-appointed judges, often referred to as the "Midnight Judges." He was nominated to be a Justice of the Peace in Washington, D.C., the lowest ranking of Adams's midnight judicial appointments. On March 4, 1801, at noon, Adams's term expired, and Jefferson was sworn in as president. The commissions of several judges, including Marbury, had not yet been officially delivered to them.

To retain firm Federalist grip on government, John Marshall served as President Adams's secretary of state nearly until Jefferson took office. On March 3, Marshall took over as chief justice of the Supreme Court. The very next day he swore in Jefferson as president.

Curiously, Chief Justice Marshall (a Federalist) and newly sworn in President Jefferson (an anti-Federalist) were not only fellow Virginia revolutionaries, they were first cousins. Despite their related blood, they were passionately split on their views of American government. The new president viewed the country as an associated group of free states in which the central government was dependent on the sum of its parts. The new chief justice, whose party was not entirely out of power, wanted a strong federal government, able to regulate the economy without consultation with or approval of the states.

In the next action of this political soap opera, the nation's new president announced that he considered the commissions of the forty-two "Midnight Judges" void, including that of the newly appointed Marbury.

This extraordinary act was justified by the fact that the commissions had not been delivered to any of the judges by the end of Adams's last day in office. James Madison was appointed by Jefferson to be secretary of state, and he was directed by Jefferson not to hand over the commissions to any of the appointees. The power struggles for the courts had now begun on both sides.

Noncommissioned, yet appointed and confirmed federal judge, Marbury took his lawsuit directly to the Supreme Court, pursuant to the Judiciary Act of 1789. Bringing the suit directly to the Supreme Court was Marbury's unknowing fatal mistake. The remedy he sought is called a *writ of mandamus*—a court order requiring a government official to carry out a nondiscretionary duty—that would have directed Madison to transmit Marbury's commission.

In the days before newspapers with photographs and personal identification cards, a newly appointed judge could only gain access to a courthouse by carrying and displaying his commission: the fancy document which confirmed his receipt of all judicial power. My commission as a judge of the Superior Court of New Jersey is today nicely framed and displayed on the wall of my office. When I was a full-time judge, I never needed it to enter the courthouse and take the bench because the sheriff's officers who secured the courthouse knew who I was. But, until the era of photographs, or without personal recognition, a judge could not take the bench without physical possession of his commission. So when Secretary of State Madison refused to deliver Marbury's commission to him, Marbury sued Madison for it.

To decide Marbury's lawsuit, the Supreme Court had to answer three questions: (1) Was Marbury entitled to his appointment?

(2) Did Marbury have a legal remedy under U.S. law? (3) Was it proper for Marbury to file his lawsuit in the Supreme Court in the first instance, or should he have filed it elsewhere?

Marbury had indeed earned a valid commission. Chief Justice Marshall said that it was effective for five years. Since he had the right to that commission, and the refusal to deliver his commission to Marbury violated his rights, there had to be a remedy for that violation.

The Court next scrutinized the 1789 law, which said the U.S. Supreme Court was indeed able to "issue writs of mandamus in cases . . . to any persons holding office under the authority of the United States."

Contrary to the new law, the Constitution itself limited the original jurisdiction of the Court—hearing and ruling on cases for the first time rather than as an appellate court—to "all cases affecting ambassadors, other public ministers and consuls, and those in which a state be a party. In all other cases the Supreme Court shall have appellate jurisdiction."

Marbury could have filed his lawsuit in the federal trial court in the nation's capital. Yet the Judiciary Act of 1789 specifically gave original jurisdiction to the Supreme Court to grant orders to people holding office under the authority of the United States, compelling them to perform a nondiscretionary ministerial duty, like delivering a valid commission to an appointed and confirmed federal judge. Congress was butting heads with the Constitution here. Can Congress give the Supreme Court *original* jurisdiction to hear a case when the Constitution did not? If it can, would not "the distribution of jurisdiction in the Constitution [be] form without substance," as Marbury famously asked. How would this conflict be resolved? Who should resolve it?

On February 24, 1803, nearly two years into Jefferson's presidency and Marbury's state of limbo, and after six days of oral argument, the Supreme Court of the United States of America held in a unanimous decision that Congress had no power to alter or enhance the Supreme Court's original jurisdiction. That meant that it found that portion of the Judiciary Act unconstitutional. Marbury was sunk. He unwittingly sued in the wrong court. Thomas Jefferson rejoiced. John Marshall lost a Federalist to the bench. But he did set a great historical precedent.

The Court reasoned that even though Marbury did have a right to his commission, and the laws do afford a remedy for the denial of that right, where the authority given to the Supreme Court by an act of Congress authorizing the Court to hear a case is not grounded in or sanctioned by the Constitution, that authority is null and void.

It was a simple but potent ruling. More than settling the political drama of the day, the high Court set forth a future hierarchy of authority for the entire United States system of government. It proclaimed that "the government is established by the Constitution and it is one of limited powers." Even though the concept of the federal government is one of "limited powers," and even though this self-evident truth is the linchpin of the opinion Chief Justice Marshall wrote for the Court, it is hard to believe that he meant what he said. As we shall see, he spent the remainder of his career finding clearly disingenuous, historically inaccurate, and highly questionable justifications for ruling that federal power is not limited.

But his words in the *Marbury* case belied his urge to centralize power. By denying that the Court had the power to hear the case because the statute that gave it that power was in conflict with the Constitution and therefore void, he shrewdly established the power of the Court to decide if such a conflict exists and to void the statute if it wishes. The powers of the legislative branch are therefore defined and limited by the Constitution, which is supreme, paramount, and superior to any legislative act. Because of this, the Court can negate any such act of Congress if it is "repugnant" to the Constitution. As Marshall saw it, Congress is only a creature created by the Constitution—it shouldn't be allowed to trump its creator.

Marbury v. Madison is the most important court decision in American history because it created *judicial review*—the power of the Supreme Court, and eventually all federal courts, to examine a statute (and eventually the behavior of the president as well) and to declare it void if the court finds it to run counter to the Constitution.

Marshall wrote that "it is the very essence of judicial duty to decide if two laws conflict, which shall supersede, and whether any law conflicts with the Constitution, which is superior and must prevail." This entire argument is brilliant, rational, and consistent with the Natural Law principle that the creature (the Congress) cannot negate acts of its creator (the Constitution).

Marshall's political genius lies in the manner in which he both expanded the Court's power and prevented a fight with his chief political opponent by serving President Jefferson's immediate interest by keeping Marbury off the bench. No one had ever argued that the Court lacked jurisdiction in this case and thereby could not force the secretary of state to commission these appointments. Surely if the Court had ordered Madison to deliver Marbury his commission, he would have done so. No one expected Jefferson to win and the Federalists to lose because the Big Government Marshall would declare that the Supreme Court actually lacked the power to hear the case and in so doing would strike down valid Federalist-enacted legislation. It was a deft move, and Marshall sharply muted any criticism of the opinion by giving Jefferson an immediate short-term victory.

But it was politically sticky for a reason not obvious at the immediate moment. Ever since this case, ruling a law or a portion of a law unconstitutional has meant that the statute no longer has the power of law, as though it never existed. In essence, this means that the Supreme Court *granted itself* the authority to declare the will of the people (as represented through the Congress) null and void if and when that will contradicts the Constitution. Here's the question: is it really for the judicial branch, and not the Congress, whose members took the same oath of office to uphold the same Constitution, to resolve conflicts between a statute and the Constitution?

In *Federalist* 78, Alexander Hamilton expounds that "A constitution is in fact, and must be, regarded by the judges as a fundamental law. It therefore belongs to them to ascertain its meaning as well as the meaning of any particular act proceeding from the legislative body." Ironically, *Marbury v. Madison* put Hamilton's notions into practice in a manner in which Jefferson, Hamilton's archrival, approved. The Court may strike down what it concludes is unconstitutional.

PUSHING *MARBURY* FURTHER

Groundbreaking as it was, the *Marbury* doctrine was extended in 1816 in the case of *Martin v. Hunter's Lessee.* Before the American Revolution, Lord Fairfax owned a huge amount of land in Virginia; but he was loyal to England, and he left the colonies during the Revolution. In 1781, when he died, his will bestowed his property to Denny Martin, his British nephew. The drama occurred from 1779 to 1785, when the State of Virginia seized land owned by non-Americans. There was not yet the Fifth Amendment to the Constitution prohibiting such seizures without compensation.

Martin's land grant from his uncle was then voided, and the State of Virginia claimed ownership to the land.

Virginia gave a portion of the land to one David Hunter. However, the Jay Treaty between Great Britain and the United States that ended the Revolutionary War guaranteed British citizens the ability to own property in America.

When the Supreme Court heard the case, it ruled that Lord Fairfax's heirs were entitled to the property, but the state court in Virginia, where the lawsuit began, declined to obey the decision of the Supreme Court. Here's the question: Could the Supreme Court extend its power of review to decisions of state courts, and thus to affirm or to reverse them? Put differently, can the Supreme Court of the United States hear an appeal from the highest court of a state on an issue—ownership of real estate—that is not even addressed in the Constitution?

The Supreme Court rejected the argument that a state government and the federal government had equal power. Writing for the Court, Justice Story applied the Constitution's Supremacy Clause (found in Article VI), which he said established the power of the Court to overrule state courts in order to maintain a consistent system of laws. As the clause states, "This Constitution, and the Laws of the United States which shall be made in Pursuance thereof; and all Treaties made, or which shall be made, under the Authority of the United States, shall be *the supreme Law of the Land;* and the Judges in every State shall be bound thereby, any Thing in the Constitution or Laws of any State to the Contrary notwithstanding." Under the Supremacy Clause, states may not pass laws in the eighteen specific, delegated, enumerated areas that have been given to Congress by the Constitution.

While the Supremacy Clause is necessary if the federal government is to have any power, it can be abused. As we shall see, the federal government can use the clause to limit the power of the states whenever it wants to regulate in a field of human behavior outside its eighteen specific, enumerated, delegated powers.

The Supreme Court—still under the leadership of Chief Justice John Marshall—reasoned that the Constitution does visit substantial disabilities, limitations, and prohibitions upon the states because they ceded away some of their powers to the federal government, and so the Founders must have contemplated that the federal judiciary would exercise appellate power over them so as to assure that they, just like the Congress, follow the Constitution. Different state courts may interpret federal laws, treaties, and even the Constitution differently, which could lead to a "deplorable state of things." And so "a national government, whose parts are subject [only] to a single Constitution, must have a single entity to give a final interpretation to its laws." And that entity can only be, the Supreme Court declared, the Supreme Court.

The Court held that the federal courts, specifically the Supreme Court, may police compliance with the Supremacy Clause and thus ensure uniform interpretation of federal laws. Here the Court expanded *Marbury*, from its power to review and void acts of Congress to its power to review and void acts of state courts for unconstitutionality.

Though these early uses of judicial review were popular at the time, they were not without critics. In *Eakin v. Raub* (1825), the Pennsylvania Supreme Court addressed whether it was authorized to consider the constitutionality of the acts of the Pennsylvania state legislature. It ruled that it could. However, Justice Gibsons's dissent in this case remains the most powerful argument against the presumed constitutionality of judicial review, as well as an indicator of why this doctrine did not soon become the constitutional "given" that it was to become years later.

Justice Gibson asked why, up until that point, this "right" claimed by the Supreme Court had not been discussed by any judge or justice other than John Marshall. He also made the following argument as to why John Marshall may have jumped to conclusions about the Supreme Court's power: "The Constitution is said to be a law of superior obligation; and consequently, that if it were to come into collision with an act of the legislature, the latter would have to give way; this is conceded. *But it is a fallacy to suppose, that they can come into collision before the judiciary.* The Constitution and the right of the legislature to pass the law, may be in collision; but is that a legitimate subject for *judicial* determination?"

Gibson continued, "If it be, the judiciary must be a peculiar organ, to revise the proceedings of the legislature, and to correct its mistakes, *and in what part of the Constitution are we to look for this proud preeminence*?" (Emphases are mine.)

Gibson also noted, "It is the business of the judiciary to interpret the laws, not scan the authority of the law giver; and without the latter, it cannot take cognizance of collision between a law and the Constitution."

In reiterating the remarks of the revered legal scholar Sir William Blackstone, Justice Gibson emphasized that democratic law expressed through acts of Congress is the will of the people and is supreme. What Gibson was saying is that without express constitutional permission giving the Supreme Court authority over Congress, the power of judicial review over congressional acts is a mere presumption on the part of Chief Justice Marshall, and a usurpation of democratic power.

Years later in reference to another decision, President Andrew Jackson would famously declare that "John Marshall has made his decision, let him go and enforce it if he can."

Marbury v. Madison may have established the judiciary's power as an equal partner among the government's branches on paper, but that holding was not universally received.

Positivists like Gibson and Jackson believed that the legislative branch could enact whatever laws it wishes. Who better to judge such matters of law than the Supreme Court of the United States of America? Who better to ensure that the liberties guaranteed in the Constitution were being upheld by the states than life-tenured judges, immune from the political winds? Who better to uphold not only constitutional rights but natural rights as well? Let's narrow down on those questions through the story of *Calder v. Bull.*

Calder v. Bull, a case decided in 1798, involved a challenge to a Connecticut law passed while a civil case was being argued in a Connecticut court. The Connecticut legislature passed a new law affecting the outcome of the civil case. The new law took property from A and gave it to B. Can you imagine the chutzpah of a state legislature peering over the shoulder of a state judge and passing laws to affect the outcome of a case the judge is trying at that moment? Unfair and unjust, right? That is exactly what the Connecticut legislature did in a case involving a sizeable amount of money. Well, the most interesting thing about *Calder* is that some of the justices considered principles of Natural Law in rendering their decision.

The Court considered a notion of immutable natural rights that the people have. The government cannot impair these rights. It is wrong for a state legislature to pass laws taking property from one person and giving it to another—a redistribution that violates the most basic ideas behind the property rights of the American free market system. Thus the Court reversed the Connecticut legislature.

Limitations on natural rights are inherent in the creation and character of the legislature itself. Natural Law implies that the rights of individual persons are the most important consideration in any case, and the Court should address them accordingly.

The *Calder* dissent sides with the Positivists in declaring that "while some have argued that a legislative act against natural justice is void, there is no court vested with the power so to declare it." That was surely so until *Marbury*, but not afterward.

JUSTLY BROWN

The Civil War and the amendments to the Constitution passed thereafter, including the Fourteenth Amendment with its "equal protection of the laws" clause, were clearly intended to end an unfortunate chapter of racial subordination and inequality in our nation. Yet equal protection in truth was a long time coming. In his dissent in *Plessey v. Ferguson*, the case that upheld the repressive "separate but equal" doctrine in public accommodations and public life, Justice John Marshall Harlan stated in 1896 that the purpose of the Civil War amendments was to make the Constitution "color blind—to remove the race line from our governmental systems." It would take nearly one hundred years after the Civil War for that to happen.

At issue in *Plessey* was a Louisiana law that was purposely crafted to ensure the superiority of whites over blacks by separating them on public trains. Justice Harlan wrote that "strict scrutiny"—meaning that the government must show to a court that its need for the law is compelling and that it has no other means of addressing that need—should be required of laws that discriminate based on race. Unfortunately, the majority did not agree and the doctrine of "separate but equal" public accommodations remained part of our legal construct for several more generations. Harlan's dissent foreshadowed the Supreme Court's decision in *Brown v. Board of Education*, which held that states could not restrict certain natural rights based on invidious racial discrimination, no matter how traditional it was.

In *Brown v. Board of Education* (1954), the Supreme Court

addressed a challenge to the segregated school system in Topeka, Kansas. The case was brought on behalf of twenty African-American students who wanted to attend an all-white public school. The Supreme Court invalidated segregated state school systems, holding that they violate the equal protection guarantee of the Fourteenth Amendment.

The briefs and arguments in this case centered upon the historical circumstances that surrounded the adoption of the Fourteenth Amendment. The Court tried to determine the intent of the amendment's authors. First, the Court asked if the drafters contemplated that the Fourteenth Amendment would abolish segregation in public schools. And, if not, does the Fourteenth Amendment embody a principle that would allow Congress (which may enforce the Fourteenth Amendment) or the judiciary (which of course may interpret the Fourteenth Amendment) to abolish segregation in public schools?

Unanimously, the Court held as a matter of law that segregation solely on the basis of race, even though tangible factors may be equal, deprives the minority group of educational opportunities. The Court reasoned that government-required racial separation generates a feeling of psychological inferiority on the numerically inferior group. That inferiority may adversely affect the mental and emotional stability of that group in ways never to be undone. This judicial finding is based upon psychiatric, anthropologic, and sociological data. Underlying the decision, though, is the Natural Law belief that all human beings must be treated equally by the government.

The strongest constitutional argument implicit in the Court's ruling (since there is no finding that the right to a free public education is a fundamental liberty) seems to be that, assuming equal facilities, the question is not one of discrimination at all but rather state impairment of the protected freedom to associate.

The freedom to associate was important to the Founders. The American Revolution began with fiery speeches and debates in public forums such as town halls and taverns. If people were not allowed to associate freely and meet with each other and discuss their ideas, then freedom of speech would be meaningless.

The Supreme Court addressed the appropriate remedy in a subsequent series of *Brown* cases. The original *Brown* decision clearly held that segregated public school systems violated the equal protection guarantee because the white schools and the black schools could not be equal. However, the Court postponed any ruling as to the relief because of the complicated nature of implementing such remedies. The Court, therefore, ordered arguments and briefs concerning the appropriate scope of its own ruling and a mechanism for granting relief.

Generally, when the Court is confronted with illegal or unconstitutional activities, it orders an immediate end to the practices. It did not do so in *Brown* due to the complexity of the case, and because of the vast effect that an immediate cessation of segregation in public schools throughout the country might bring about.

The Court did not order that all schools be integrated, it ordered only that the intentionally segregated school systems be dismantled "with all deliberate speed." The only immediate requirement was "a prompt and reasonable 'start' toward full compliance"; once the "start" had been made, school authorities could be granted more time to comply if the time was necessary in order to serve the public good and the delay was consistent with good faith compliance and public safety.

The general authority and responsibility for supervising the transition from a dual to a unified school system was conferred on the federal district courts. However, neither *Brown* nor the litigation that followed it (*Brown II* and its progeny) required all public schools to be racially integrated. Rather, the decisions have required that public schools not be intentionally racially segregated by law. It did not outlaw segregation resulting from housing patterns or other personal choices.

This distinction is between *de jure* and *de facto. De jure* means "by law." This would mean segregation stemming from some purposeful act of governmental authorities. *De facto* means "by fact," and would be segregation that occurs because of demographic patterns, unconnected to any purposeful governmental action intended to segregate racially. *Brown* and its progeny mandate the correction only of *de jure* segregation.

Rather than address Natural Law rights directly, the *Brown* Court appeared to be more comfortable discussing the Fourteenth Amendment. The notion of due process is vague enough to permit the Court to invalidate laws that are abhorrent to the basic rights of men and women, namely Natural Law.

So why are *Marbury* and *Brown* (and to a lesser extent *Martin* and *Calder*) among the most important stories in constitutional history? Why is it that every American should be intimately familiar with them? The reason is that they finally establish the power of the Supreme Court, and thus all federal courts, to prevent the president, the Congress, and the states, by law or custom, from violating the Constitution or the Natural Law.

But how has the Court used, and refused to exercise, that power? That is the subject we take up next.

3

CONGRESSIONAL POWER GRAB

Banking on Government Growth

With his bias for centralized government, Supreme Court Chief Justice John Marshall started the ball rolling down the Big Government hill from the earliest days of the republic. *Marbury v. Madison* proved to be a mixed bag. On the upside, it cemented the principle of judicial review, which allowed judges to invalidate laws that violate citizens' natural rights. On the downside, it gave incredible trumping power to the Supreme Court. But *Marbury* could only go so far. An obscure 1819 case helped expand federal power much further.

The case was *McCulloch v. Maryland.* The decision dramatically expanded the scope of congressional authority and the power of the federal government. The Supreme Court's opinion in this case cemented the creation of a leviathan-like federal government, far larger and more expansive than the Founders had created just thirty years earlier. It broadened the powers of the federal government through Congress, and it narrowed the power of the states.

At issue was whether Congress could charter a bank. Alexander Hamilton, who was then secretary of the treasury and an advocate of bigger government, proposed to Congress in 1791 that it charter a central bank for the United States to implement and fulfill his financial policies.

Thomas Jefferson, then the secretary of state, objected. He argued that Congress did not have an enumerated power in the Constitution that authorized it to create a bank. Under his conception of a limited federal government, Congress could not exercise powers other than those that the states clearly gave it. Establishing such a bank would necessarily sap authority from state governments. Hamilton responded by flipping the argument on its head; as he saw it, the powers of Congress should be everything except what the Constitution explicitly prohibits.

To support this argument, he cited the Necessary and Proper Clause of Article I, Section 8, Clause 18, of the U.S. Constitution. As we saw in chapter two, the eighteenth specific, delegated, enumerated power, the qualifier, confers on Congress the ability to pass legislation to fulfill the previous "enumerated powers" granted in Clauses 1 through 17. These seventeen clauses contain specific powers that the Constitution gives to the federal government. Clause 18, however, grants Congress what some have argued is a broader power. It states that Congress has the power "To make all Laws which shall be *necessary and proper* for carrying into Execution the foregoing Powers, and all other Powers vested by this Constitution in the Government of the United States, or in any Department or Officer thereof."

The "loose constructionists" (at the time Hamilton's Federalists) saw in Clause 18 a chance to strengthen the federal government. The "strict constructionists" (at the time Jefferson's anti-Federalists[1]) believed that Clause 18 actually curtailed federal power.

MORE POWER TO YOU

The anti-Federalists interpreted "necessary and proper" as meaning whatever was "essential" or "indispensable." Their opponents interpreted it to mean anything that was "helpful" to achieve a constitutional purpose. Both views are gone now. Today what is "necessary and proper" is typically anything that the federal government wants it to be.

The strict constructionists truly believed that Congress could perform only those particular functions articulated in Clauses 1 through 17. To interpret this in a different way would violate the clear language of the Tenth Amendment, which declares that any powers not given to the federal government are left to the states and the people. This amendment defies and repudiates Hamilton's argument—but Hamilton had an important backer.

In the creation of a federal bank, President Washington supported Hamilton. At his urging, Congress established the Bank of the United States, complete with a twenty-year charter.

The Jeffersonians, who were in power by the dawn of the nineteenth century, did not renew the charter when it expired in 1811. But then came the War of 1812, and the federal government was in need of a financial pick-me-up. President Madison, who had opposed the first bank, thought a central bank would help the financially strapped government. At his suggestion, in 1816, Congress commissioned a second Bank of the United States, which soon opened branches throughout the country.

Then things got complicated.

Many state and private banks were anxious to follow their own independent policies and were offended by the overreaching regulations of the federal Bank. The states looked to their respective legislatures to limit the operations of the central Bank.

Maryland's legislature wanted to protect its state-chartered banks, so it tried to tax the federal Bank. James McCulloch, an employee in the Baltimore branch of the federal Bank, refused to pay the state tax; so Maryland sued him. This put state and federal power in a direct contest, the outcome of which would have profound effects on the nature of American government.

The attorney for the Bank claimed that Maryland could not tax it because the states only have the power to tax their constituents, and an instrumentality of the United States is not a constituent of a state. Maryland claimed that the Bank was not an instrumentality of the United States because Congress did not have the power to create it in the first place. The power to establish a bank is not listed in the enumerated powers of Article I, Section 8.

Ah, but then there is that Necessary and Proper Clause. Maryland argued that "necessary and proper" meant that Congress could *only* do what was necessary and proper to carry out its other enumerated powers; the phrase limits the power of Congress rather than expands it. That's not how the Supreme Court saw the matter when it decided *McCulloch v. Maryland.* The Court sided with the Bank and expanded federal powers. It held that there was an inherent limitation on the power of states to tax instruments of the federal government.

Chief Justice Marshall's opinion considered two major questions. The second question was whether the states had the right to tax the Bank. The first question was whether Congress had the authority to create the Bank of the United States in the first place. Chief Justice Marshall championed the Federalist position and decided that Congress did have the power to create a national bank through what has come to be known as Congress's *implied powers.* Just as he did in *Marbury v. Madison,* in establishing broad judicial powers, Chief Justice Marshall not only endorsed the constitutionality of the Bank, but he articulated a broad notion of federal power and paved the way for the present-day welfare state that grew after the Civil War.

The crucial difference between *Marbury* and *McCulloch* was that *Marbury* and judicial review are needed to keep the Congress from expanding the federal government in defiance of the Constitution, while expansive use of the Necessary and Proper Clause, endorsed in *McCulloch,* does just the opposite.

THE SUPREME FEDERAL GOVERNMENT

Marshall rejected the argument that the states retain ultimate sovereignty because they ratified the Constitution and therefore have the authority to veto federal actions not specifically authorized by the Constitution, such as the creation of a federal bank. Marshall wrote that it was the people who ratified the Constitution, and they were thus sovereign, not the states.

That was both historically incorrect and intellectually dishonest. Marshall simply did whatever he wanted to enlarge and strengthen the big central government. His one correct decision on judicial review, *Marbury,* just happened to fit with his desire to enlarge federal power, not really to keep it in check, as the Founders expected. In *McCulloch,* Marshall wrote that the Constitutional Convention created a social compact between the federal government and *individual Americans.* The federal government, Marshall claimed, arises from the citizens, not the states, and binds the states. In this view, states are not a check on the Congress. This is the linchpin in the Federalists' argument for federal supremacy.

Marshall's argument was rhetorically powerful and had a certain appeal during this critical and early stage of the Union. But his reasoning was deeply flawed. Says Article VII of the Constitution, "The Ratification of the Conventions of nine States shall be sufficient for the Establishment of this Constitution between the States so ratifying the Same." The Constitution was not approved by the people in the form of a national plebiscite. It was ratified *by the states.* According to the document itself, the states had to ratify the Constitution, not the people. But there was more to Marshall's argument.

He did admit that the Constitution did not explicitly empower Congress with the right to create a Bank. But he said that that alone did not prohibit it. Marshall argued that Congress may act under either explicit powers or *implied* powers that the Constitution grants to it. Although the term "bank" is not in the list of constitutionally granted congressional powers, other things such as collecting taxes, borrowing money, and regulating commerce are included. Therefore, Congress can create a Bank in order to effectuate those powers. He reasoned that it is simply not possible to list every conceivable power needed in the present or future in such a document.

In summarizing this premise, Marshall wrote what has been described as the single most important sentence in constitutional literature: "In considering this question we must never forget that this is a *Constitution* we are expounding." By this Marshall meant that this was a document that encompassed the guidelines for a nation. This document was meant to live, breathe, and guide for future generations. It was not a simple statute or an ordinance that stated specific rules of law.

Where did he get this stuff? Certainly not in the text of the founding documents. His argument here is as novel and original as was his rationale in *Marbury.* Marshall concluded that Congress has the right to choose *any* means not prohibited by the Constitution to carry out its broad powers. This was a dramatic expansion of the scope of congressional authority. If Congress can choose *any* means not prohibited by the Constitution to carry out its own powers, it truly has an almost infinite range of options that could be carried into law.

TORTURING THE NECESSARY AND PROPER CLAUSE

Marshall adopted this view of congressional power even before he turned to the Necessary and Proper Clause for support. He took the loose constructionist view of the clause by allowing Congress to pursue a goal that is "rationally related" to the enumerated powers, as long as the Constitution does not prohibit it. *What is rationally related?* Just about anything, as we will see later, became "rationally related."

In another profound sentence from the *McCulloch* opinion, Marshall wrote, "let the ends be legitimate, let it be within the scope of the Constitution, and all means which are appropriate, which are plainly adapted to that end, which are not prohibited, but are consistent with the letter and spirit of the Constitution, are Constitutional."

How could the chief justice make such an unconstitutional argument? How could the same mind that declared the federal government one of limited powers—so limited it could not allow William Marbury to file his lawsuit in the Supreme Court because the Constitution did not authorize it—just a few years later give the Congress a blank check to write virtually any laws it wanted so long as they were "rationally related" to a power granted in the Constitution?

Marshall certainly knew better. His statements of that which "are not prohibited" by the document clash with his previously discussed statements that the Constitution created a limited federal government. The chief justice claimed that one cannot possibly see all the future prohibitions and laws needed, yet he wanted things to be "consistent with the letter and the spirit of the Constitution." But both the letter *and* the spirit of the Constitution require a government of limited powers.

The Founders did *not* intend for the Constitution to be twisted and modified for the day. They gave a lot of forethought to the psychology and history of the ways of mankind.

Marshall refused to treat the Necessary and Proper Clause as a *limit* on congressional power. He rejected the view that it allows Congress to adopt only those laws which are truly "necessary," meaning "indispensable," which is how the term is used in other parts of constitutional law.

The word "necessary" has become a term of art in constitutional jurisprudence. For example, when the government engages in discrimination based on race or when it interferes with a fundamental right, the government can prevail *only* if its action is *necessary* to achieve a compelling interest. "Necessary" in this context means "essential" to achieve a certain goal. To support his broad meaning of the word "necessary," Marshall argued that since the clause is listed in Article I, Section 8, which expands the powers of Congress, not the sections that limit Congress, it further enlarges the powers of the government.

But the chief justice did admit that the powers granted to Congress are not limitless. He then boosted the power of the judiciary over that of Congress. He explained that "should Congress, in the execution of its powers, adopt measures which are prohibited by the Constitution; or should Congress, under the pretext of executing its powers, pass laws for the accomplishment of objects not entrusted to the [federal] government, it would become the painful duty of this tribunal . . . to say, that such an act is not the law of the land."

But wait: isn't that exactly what Congress did in creating a national Bank?

The chief justice held that a state's laws must not be at odds with the Constitution and must yield to it if there is a variance. Because the "power to tax involves the power to destroy," Marshall concluded that the State of Maryland's tax of the federal government's bank was invalid. If states could tax the Bank, they could ruin nearly any federal action and contravene the Supremacy Clause of the Constitution. Marshall concluded that the federal government had the power to create the Bank, but it was impermissible for Maryland to tax it, and the Court declared the tax unconstitutional. He was wrong on the first count, which led us down the slippery slope of Big Government expansion. Here it was accomplished by twisting the definition of "necessary and proper." Later, it will be under the guise of regulation of interstate commerce.

IN THE TANK

Since Marshall, what has Congress done under the cloak of its necessary and proper powers? It has set speed limits, limited the size of toilet bowls and the water pressure of showerheads, and tried to scrutinize the content of the urine of professional athletes, among other things. If only Congress understood the eighteen enumerated powers and respected the Natural Law!

Natural Law provides an objective standard of right and wrong. But it is essential to distinguish the objective wrongness of an act from the subjective culpability, if any, of the person who does it. Professor Rice puts it best when he writes that Natural Law "serves as a standard for the laws enacted by the state. If an enacted law is contrary to the natural law, it is not even a law. It is void, an act of violence rather than law. The natural law is therefore a standard for the state as well as for its citizens."

The following are a few examples of congressional overreaching that resulted in Positivist laws that intrude into aspects of daily life never envisioned by the Founders.

Let's start with federal regulation of toilet bowls. The Energy Policy and Conservation Act of 1992 establishes a maximum amount of water that can be used by toilets and showers in private homes. Toilets cannot use more than 1.6 gallons per flush. The act codified standards for the size and maximum amount of water to be used in American toilets.[2] Thus, an individual is in violation of the law if he installs in his home a toilet that is larger or uses more water than provided for in the guidelines. Showers are limited to 2.5 gallons per minute. These ridiculous federal regulations of private individual behavior were put in place nationally, even in places where there is an abundance of water. Installing items that do not meet these standards can result in a fine of $2,500.

The Energy Policy and Conservation Act was intended "to conserve water by improving the water efficiency of certain plumbing products and appliances." But many states adopted their own water-flow standards prior to federal enactment of this policy, which is precisely why states should be left to their own wills and needs to decide what is best for them locally.

The 102nd Congress's Congressional Record suggests that the primary justification for the Energy Policy Act is our continued over-consumption of, and dependence on, foreign oil. Almost all of the discussion by proponents of the bill centered on the need for alternative sources of renewable energy. There was one mention of water in the entire record, despite the inclusion of the burdensome requirements. There was no mention of a water shortage, and no mention of the Constitution.

Moreover, the standards are ineffective in conserving water, because the reduction in water flow has resulted in poor toilet performance, requiring multiple flushes to evacuate its contents!

The Water Resources Research Center at the University of Arizona undertook a study (funded in part by the regional Bureau of Reclamation and the City of Phoenix) to assess the viability of the new toilets.[3] Preliminary findings suggested clogging, the need for multiple flushes, and other problems with the functioning of "low-consumption" toilets.

Problems increase as the toilets age. While Congress regulated "gallons per flush," it neglected to regulate the mechanism by which the flushing is accomplished, and the use of previously existing technology with the new bowls seems to create the problems. In addition, the mechanism permits more water volume per flush than intended, so a number (26.5 percent) of the studied low-consumption toilets average 2.2 gallons of water per flush. Regulations not working? What a surprise considering the expert congressional "do-gooders" who know everything. There may be a black market for imported toilets.

So all of this is necessary and proper to serve just which of Congress's enumerated powers?

PATRIOTIC PEEPING TOMS

The USA PATRIOT Act, particularly Section 215, permits the FBI to obtain "tangible materials" (e.g., records, files, etc.) about a particular person from a third party without a search warrant authorized by a judge.

As mentioned earlier, the American colonists were subject to many searches and seizures under British rule. British soldiers could search anyone's home at any time without limitation because Parliament authorized them to do so. This behavior was fresh in the minds of the Founders when they drafted an amendment designed to prevent these infractions on personal liberties.

The Fourth Amendment was designed to protect citizens from unreasonable searches and seizures. By requiring a warrant issued by a judge and by requiring the judge to find that the person whose property or records are being sought more likely than not has committed a crime before a search can take place, the Constitution provides persons with protection from arbitrary and unfettered government searches. The Founders intended that no person should be subject to searches and seizures of his private property unless the government presented evidence to a judge, who then issued a warrant. The evidence presented must establish probable cause that a crime has been committed before a warrant can be issued.

Under Section 215 of the PATRIOT Act, the FBI can ask librarians, booksellers, or Internet providers to disclose information about the materials being accessed by a particular client.[4] The "order" or request from the FBI need not disclose the nature of the investigation for which it is being requested.

Worse, the provider of the information is forbidden from disclosing the request to anyone except those persons needed to obtain the information, including management personnel. A person who produces these "tangible things" in compliance with an FBI "order" will not be deemed to have waived any privilege vis-à-vis the subject of the investigation.

While the First Amendment protects free speech and the freedom of the press, the Ninth Amendment states that the enumeration of certain powers in the Constitution does not limit the power of the people. The PATRIOT Act interferes with both of these amendments by allowing federal agents to obtain confidential information in excess of the powers given to the federal government.

Whatever its perceived merits in the war on terror, the PATRIOT Act is a lawless law because it allows the federal government to obtain information without a warrant, thus violating the Fourth Amendment, and it quashes speech in violation of the First

Amendment, and overreaches the scope of federal power in violation of the Ninth Amendment.

CENSUS SNOOPING

In 2000, Sen. Trent Lott (R-Mississippi), and other Republicans, "shocked" by the number of calls that they received about the intrusiveness of the Census Bureau's long form questionnaire, urged citizens to decline to answer questions that violated their privacy. The real shocker in this story is that Congress approved the entire questionnaire, apparently without reading it!

The more controversial questions asked about respondents' mental and emotional health status (specifically, whether any persons with these concerns lived in the household, and whether their condition made it difficult for them to eat, bathe, etc.) and whether the home had a shower and a flush toilet. President Bush said that he would not necessarily answer all of the questions posed by the Census Bureau. (So why did he allow those idiotic bureaucrats who work in the executive branch of the federal government, of which he is the head, to ask those questions in the first place?)

The Constitution authorizes a census "in such a manner as they [the Congress] shall by law direct." The constitutional authority is broad, but the question is whether broad authority allows such intrusion into the personal lives of citizens.[5] Because the compelled answers to these questions invade constitutionally protected areas of privacy, such intrusion cannot be constitutional.

BIG BROTHER IS WATCHING TELEVISION

In 2003, the Federal Communications Commission promulgated a regulation that would require all High Definition TV (HDTV) sets sold after July 1, 2005, to be installed with antipiracy software, i.e., a "broadcast flag."[6] The U.S. Court of Appeals for the District of Columbia Circuit struck down the provision in May 2005. The court said that Congress would have to enact such a provision, and the FCC exceeded the scope of its authority by doing so.

Congress may elect to mandate antipiracy software in response to growing demands from the entertainment lobby. If it does, this is like having a government official on your television to tell you whether you may record programming and watch it later. The FCC is regulating what people do with programming "after it has entered their homes." Is this permissible? Of course not.

More than twenty years ago in the *Sony Corp v. Universal Studios* case, the United States Supreme Court ruled that taping televised programs on a Sony Betamax (remember them?) or VCR constituted nothing more than "time shifting," which was a fair use of the programming and not a violation of copyright law. HDTV sets and personal video recorders may be a new technology, but the fair use issue remains the same.

There is no need for the FCC or Congress—driven by entertainment industry lobbyists—to infringe on our right to view televised programming at home at our chosen time. The government has no legitimate business inside our televisions.

THE BEAT GOES ON

I could go on all day with examples of government overreaching and abuse of the Necessary and Proper Clause, all supposedly done for the general welfare.

There have been many bizarre examples of congressional pork, many of which can be found in the 2003 Omnibus Spending Bill. Rep. Jeff Flake (R-Arizona) issues weekly press releases that detail many of these monstrosities:

- Congress allotted $200,000 for the American Cotton Museum. (Why should people in New York City pay for a cotton museum in Alabama?)
- Congress allotted $70,000 for the International Paper Industry Hall of Fame in Appleton, Wisconsin.
- Congress allotted $150,000 for the Therapeutic Horseback Riding Program at the Lady B Ranch in California. (Does Hillary Clinton's 1992 Health Care Reform Act cover this?)
- Congress allotted $1.5 million to transport cold water to Lake Onondaga from Lake Ontario. (Why on earth are we doing this?)
- Congress allocated $160,000 for seafood waste in Alaska. (I hope they mean *cleanup* of seafood waste.)
- Congress promised $75,000 for the Greater Syracuse Sports Hall of Fame. (And where is this in the Constitution?)
- Congress gave $99,000 to train students in the motor sports industry at Patrick Henry Community College. (Is motor sporting a natural right?)
- Congress voted $250,000 to build and renovate city pools in Banning, California. (The next time it's hot in your neighborhood, why don't you go to California for a swim to cool down? After all, you paid for this.)

Republicans used to mock Democrats for inserting questionable provisions into government spending bills. Now that the Republicans control Congress, they have passed similar measures. One bill was worth over $328 billion, and contained appropriations for several government agencies. The spending bill was filled with nearly seven thousand questionable spending provisions.[7] Did your congressperson and senators read this claptrap before voting on it? Not likely.

The state of pork spending and overregulation by Congress has reached such an extreme that it would almost be laughable if it weren't so sad. These are *our lives* that members of Congress are regulating. This is *our money* they are burning on special projects in their home districts.

The Constitution—and the eighteen specific limited, enumerated powers given to Congress—did not give such an enormous grant of power to Congress. In large part, we have Chief Justice John Marshall to blame for getting this giant ball of federal power rolling in *McCulloch.*

It's been downhill since.

4

DISHONEST ABE

The Lincoln You Didn't Know

The Abraham Lincoln of legend is an honest man who freed the slaves and saved the Union.

Few things could be more misleading.

In order to increase his federalist vision of centralized power, "Honest" Abe misled the nation into an unnecessary war. He claimed that the war was about emancipating slaves, but he could have simply paid slave owners to set their slaves free. The benefits of the Union would have been fairly easy to see once a few Southern states tried to go it alone for a bit. But Lincoln chose not to compensate slave owners and thereby end the dreaded institution. Instead he chose to deny states their right to participate voluntarily in the Union.

The bloodiest war in American history could have been avoided. But, with very little regard for honesty, Lincoln increased federal power and assaulted the Constitution.

His actions were unconstitutional, and he knew it. Before running for president, Lincoln was quoted as saying that the Southern states would not be permitted to secede (not, significantly, that they did not have a *right* to secede). By barring their departure, Lincoln preserved the geographical Union but tore apart the Constitution. He blatantly ignored the rights of the states to secede from the Union, a right that is clearly implicit in the Constitution, since it was the *states* that ratified the Constitution and thereby decided to enter the Union. Surely these same states had the right to decide to undo that act.

Lincoln's view was a far departure from the approach of Thomas Jefferson, who recognized states' rights above those of the Union. In fact, Jefferson said that the federal government was legitimate only if it served state interests (because Jefferson, like his successor Ronald Reagan, understood that the states created the federal government), and the right of secession was a given. After all, Jefferson reasoned, the act of joining the Union—of ratifying the Constitution—was a simple state legislative act. And cannot any legislature rewrite its own laws? Of course it can.

THE RIGHT TO TAKE A WALK

One need look no further than the Declaration of Independence for exposition of a "moral" right to secede, which every single one of the colonies acknowledged by signing the document.

The first paragraph of the Declaration of Independence begins, "When in the Course of human Events it becomes necessary for one People to dissolve the Political Bands which have connected them with another and to assume among the Powers of the Earth, the separate and equal Station to which the Laws of Nature and of Nature's God entitle them, a decent Respect to the Opinions of Mankind requires that they should declare the causes which impel them to the Separation." In other words, the right to secede from any confederation, group, or union is derived from the Natural Law of freedom to associate.

The text goes on to argue that "when a long Train of Abuses and Usurpations, pursuing invariably the same Object evinces a design to reduce them under absolute Despotism, it is their Right, it is their Duty, to throw off such Government, and to provide new Guards for their future Security." The right to secede is implicit.

The Ninth and Tenth Amendments to the Constitution have been interpreted as incorporating the values espoused in the Declaration, which reserve the powers not given to the federal government to the people and the states. In fact, several states would not have ratified a Constitution that denied them the right to secede—that is, to withdraw peacefully—if things did not go well under the new government.

During the Constitutional Convention, a provision was proposed that would have permitted the federal government to use force against a state that did not comply with congressional mandates. Edmund Randolph, a delegate to the Constitutional Convention from Virginia, presented his "Virginia Plan," which provided that the government could use force against states of the union that neglected to fulfill their obligations.

Much of the Virginia Plan was adopted into the Constitution, but the provision allowing for the use of force by the government against the states was conspicuously omitted. If states continued to recognize the right to secede, which they clearly did, one is left to wonder why it was so vehemently opposed by Lincoln and his troops.

The Confiscation Acts were two separate laws passed by Congress in 1861 and 1862. The acts dealt with freeing slaves from the Confederacy. These acts set the stage for the Emancipation Proclamation. As the Union army invaded portions of the South, the soldiers encountered many slaves. Some were fugitive slaves from other parts of the Confederacy, while others were living on captured estates. Union army commanders did not know what to do with these slaves, so Congress responded with the Confiscation Acts. Some army officers freed the slaves they encountered and provided them with supplies and a start to a new life in the North. Other army officers, many of whose units had limited supplies, sent slaves back to their masters in the South. The army simply did not have the means to care for them.

Congress addressed the differing behavior of army officers when it passed the Confiscation Acts. The Confiscation Act of 1862 stated that any slaves behind Union lines were captives of war who were to be freed.

These newly freed slaves were not to be housed in the North, though. The act provided that slaves would be transported to countries in the tropics. The idea was that slaves would be returned to their countries of origin or at least moved elsewhere.

The Confiscation Acts show that Lincoln did not have much concern for the slaves. He did not suggest to Congress that freed slaves should be granted civil rights or citizenship in Northern states. Once the freed slaves were transported out of the United States, they would no longer be Lincoln's problem.

It is important to note that only slaves from states in open rebellion were to be freed by the Union army. If a fugitive slave escaped from a border state to the North, then the slave would be returned to the "owner." All that the "owner" had to do was show his loyalty to the Union. Lincoln did not want to risk alienating the border states. He believed that Tennessee and Virginia could be persuaded to leave the Confederacy and join the Union again if federal troops returned fugitive slaves to their "owners" in those states, and was willing to do so.

The Confiscation Acts appear to have been passed in the spirit of freedom and justice, but a closer examination reveals that Congress was merely reacting to a question presented by Union army officers.

Lincoln was interested in these acts only as far as they were able to persuade states to buy into his idea of a large federal government. If slaves were truly property, the feds could have seized and paid for them. But slaves were truly human, possessing inalienable natural rights. So why did Lincoln wage two-and-a-half years of bloody war before freeing them?

FEET OF CLAY

Lincoln liked to think of himself as continuing the political philosophy of Henry Clay, who had been the leader of the Whigs.

For forty years, Clay supported the creation of an American empire through measures such as corporate welfare (which politicians liked to call "internal improvements"); today we call them corporate tax breaks, protectionist tariffs, and a nationwide central bank. All of the things that Clay favored in essence provided for a highly centralized government. And Lincoln supported them all.

The Civil War years saw the rapid centralization and enlargement of the federal government. Taxes were imposed upon most manufactured goods, tariff rates were increased, and an inheritance tax was adopted. During this period, the first personal income tax in the history of the United States was imposed, even though Article I, Section 9 of the Constitution stated, "No capitation, or other direct Tax, shall be laid unless in Proportion to the Census or Enumeration." The highest rate was 10 percent for people with incomes over $10,000 per year.[1]

Stephen Douglas portrayed Lincoln as desiring to "impose on the nation a uniformity of local laws and institutions and a moral homogeneity dictated by the central government" that "placed at defiance the intentions of the republic's Founders."[2]

The Lincoln-Douglas debate dialogue was a "contest all over again between the 'one consolidated empire' of the Federalists and Whigs, and the 'confederacy of sovereign and equal states' of Jefferson and Jackson."[3] Douglas argued that "Lincoln goes for consolidation and uniformity in our government, while I go for maintaining the confederation of the sovereign states."[4]

In his 1831 Fort Hill Address, John C. Calhoun, then serving as vice president under President Andrew Jackson, declared: "stripped of all its covering, the naked question is, whether ours is a federal or consolidated government; a constitutional or absolute one; a government resting solidly on the basis of sovereignty of the States, or the unrestrained will of the majority; a form of government, as in all other unlimited ones, in which injustice, violence, and force must ultimately prevail."[5]

Federalism has been called one of the greatest contributions of the Founding Fathers to the field of government. Lincoln single handedly voided that contribution. Professor Thomas DiLorenzo has said that "the federal government will never check its own power. That is the whole reason for federalism and the reason that the founding fathers adopted a federal system of government. . . . There is no check on the federal government unless state sovereignty exists, and state sovereignty is itself meaningless without the right of secession. Thus Lincoln's war, by destroying the right of secession, also destroyed the last check on the potentially tyrannical power of the central state."[6] And DiLorenzo is correct. Lincoln destroyed federalism through the Civil War.

LINCOLN AS LIBERATOR

Lincoln's act of sending troops to Virginia triggered the armed conflict that became the Civil War. He did so under the premise that war was necessary to preserve the Union. But the truth is that Lincoln had several other options to exhaust before resorting to warfare—and that's only after we observe that the Southern states had the right to secede from the Union if they wished to do so.

In his Inaugural Address, Jefferson declared, "If there be any among us who would wish to dissolve this Union or to change its republican form, let them stand undisturbed as monuments of the safety with which error of opinion may be tolerated where reason is left free to combat it."[7]

Should some states want to secede, "God bless them both and keep them in the union if it be for their good, but separate them if it be better," he said during his presidency.[8]

Before dispatching troops to the south, Lincoln had not expressed any intent to make blacks equal with whites. In a debate with Stephen Douglas on September 18, 1858, he said, "I will say then that I am not, nor ever have been in favor of bringing about in any way the social and political equality of the white and black races—that I am not nor ever have been in favor of making voters or jurors of Negroes."

When Lincoln issued the Emancipation Proclamation in 1863, most Northerners were surprised because the government had never previously said that the reason for the war was to liberate black slaves in the South.

By the time of the Civil War, many foreign countries had ended slavery peacefully. England had freed its slaves without a violent conflict about twenty years earlier. Gradual emancipation would be successful in the Dutch colonies (1863), Puerto Rico (1873), Brazil (1871–88), and Cuba (1886).[9]

To this day, the Civil War has the distinction of having the highest death toll of American citizens of any conflict in which the United States has been a part. There were more than 620,000 deaths, many thousands of people were left crippled, and nearly 40 percent of the nation's economy had been destroyed. In hindsight, most Americans in both the North and South would probably have supported a peaceful method of freeing the slaves rather than a long, costly war.

When he became president, Lincoln claimed that he did not intend to interfere with slavery in the Southern states, and he even went as far as saying that it would be unconstitutional for him to do so. Lincoln's compromises on the issue of slavery brought criticism from Northern abolitionists.[10]

The only military action that Lincoln spoke of in his First Inaugural Address was sending federal troops to states disregarding tariff laws. "The power confided in me will be used to hold, occupy, and possess the property, and places belonging to the government, and to collect the duties and imposts; but beyond what may be necessary for these objects, there will be no invasion—no using force against, or among the people anywhere."[11] Lincoln was more concerned about the failure of states to collect tariffs than he was about slavery.

UNLIKELY DICTATOR

Lincoln managed to end the right of secession forever. In the process, a large number of civil liberties were trampled, prompting historians Henry S. Commager and Samuel Morison to call Lincoln "a dictator from the standpoint of American Constitutional law and practice." Even Lincoln supporters like James F. Rhodes accused him of being a dictator. Yet Rhodes noted that "never had the power of dictator fallen into safer and nobler hands." James G. Randall said that "if Lincoln was a dictator, it must be admitted that he was a benevolent dictator."[12] The numerous civilians who were injured by Lincoln's troops, the citizens whose homes were burned and destroyed, and the parents and wives who lost their loved ones in the Civil War would certainly not have called him a "benevolent dictator."

As DiLorenzo has observed,

> [H]ad the South been permitted to go in peace, as was the wish of the majority of the Northern opinion makers before Fort Sumter according to historian Joseph Perkins, a democracy would have continued to thrive in the two nations. Moreover, the act of secession would have had exactly the effect the founding fathers expected it to have; it would have tempered the imperialistic proclivities of the central state. The federal government would have been forced to moderate its high-tariff policies and to slow down or abandon its quest for empire. Commercial relationships with the South would have continued and expanded. After a number of years, the same reasons that led colonists to form a Union in the first place would likely have become more appealing to both sections, and the Union would probably have been reunited.[13]

The most egregious violations of civil liberties that Lincoln committed were murdering civilians, declaring martial law, suspending habeas corpus, seizing vast amounts of private property without compensation (including railroads and telegraphs), conducting a war without the consent of Congress, imprisoning nearly thirty thousand *Northern* citizens without trial, shutting down several newspapers, and even deporting a congressman (Clement L. Vallandigham from Ohio) because he objected to the imposition of an income tax.[14] Members of Congress from the Republican

Party who were associated with Lincoln tampered with the Electoral College by creating the new states of Nevada, Kansas, and West Virginia in order to secure Lincoln's victory in the 1864 election.[15]

In Maryland alone, Lincoln's troops arrested and imprisoned without trial a mayor, a congressman, and thirty-one state legislators. Even Francis Scott Key's grandson was not spared.[16] Lincoln took all of these actions in the name of *preserving* constitutional government. It is hard to imagine something more tyrannical than a central government that suppresses life, speech, and political expression with such drastic measures.[17]

When Abraham Lincoln organized a militia in April 1861, the Civil War began. Lincoln took action and made important decisions to further military operations. He greatly expanded the army and navy and used federal money to purchase arms and ammunition.

Lincoln did all of this without the consent of Congress. He claimed that he was suppressing a rebellion, but what he was doing was fomenting a rebellion and fighting an undeclared war. And only Congress can declare war.

Of all his constitutionally dubious activities, Lincoln's determination to suspend *habeas corpus* was the most egregious and controversial. He issued a proclamation on September 24, 1862, that implemented martial law and suspended *habeas corpus.*

A writ of *habeas corpus* is a judicial order that directs prison officials to facilitate an inmate's appearance at a judicial proceeding wherein a judge will determine whether the prisoner has been lawfully imprisoned or whether he should be released. Someone who objects to being detained can bring a petition for *habeas corpus.* The right is guaranteed in the Constitution unless suspended by the Congress in time of rebellion.

In *McCleskey v. Kemp* (1987), the Supreme Court called *habeas corpus* "one of the centerpieces of our liberties." The fact that Lincoln suspended *habeas corpus* demonstrates that he was willing to tread on civil liberties in order to advance his political objectives.

John Merryman was a confederate sympathizer from Maryland and a vocal opponent of the Union. He apparently recruited soldiers to serve in the Confederate Army. Merryman was arrested by the Union Army for conspiring to organize the overthrow of the U.S. government. Merryman petitioned the U.S. Supreme Court for a writ of *habeas corpus.* Chief Justice Roger Taney granted the writ, meaning he ordered the government to bring Merryman into his courtroom and legally justify his confinement.

However, President Lincoln suspended the writ of *habeas corpus,* and military officials refused to produce Merryman for proceedings in the Supreme Court. Chief Justice Taney wrote an opinion, *Ex Parte Merryman,* in which he clearly stated that only Congress had the power to suspend *habeas corpus.*

Chief Justice Taney wrote that the president essentially has only one power regarding the life, liberty, and property of private citizens. The president has the power to "take care that the laws shall be faithfully executed." The president "is not authorized to execute them himself, or through agents or officers, civil or military, appointed by himself, but he is to take care that they be faithfully carried into execution, as they are expounded and adjudged by the coordinate branch of the government to which that duty is assigned by the constitution."

Taney wrote that "If the president of the United States may suspend the writ, then the constitution of the United States has conferred upon him more regal and absolute power over the liberty of the citizen."

DiLorenzo stated that "after suspension of *habeas corpus* had been an accomplished fact for some time, and thousands of arrests had been made, the Republican-controlled Congress finally got around to rubber-stamping the suspension. Taney had issued his opinion as part of his duties as a circuit court judge, a duty Supreme Court justices had at the time. The Lincoln administration never bothered to appeal his decision to a higher court, but just ignored it."[18]

Taney also challenged Lincoln's notion that the situation at hand required him to use his authority as commander in chief to take "any measure" that would suppress "the enemy."[19] Was preservation of the Union an imminent enough concern to justify suspending constitutionally guaranteed freedoms?

This was one of the justifications Abraham Lincoln gave for his actions. Chief Justice Taney, however, held that were Lincoln's interpretation of *his* powers correct, the Constitution would be moot because the executive branch could usurp the power of all the other branches of government. The Founders clearly could not have intended such a result, because they limited the power of the president.

While the Constitution provides that the writ may be suspended "in cases of rebellion and when the public safety" necessitates, it is clear that only Congress may suspend it. The power is in Article I of the Constitution, which sets forth the powers of Congress, and Chief Justice Taney thought that this supported his conclusion that Congress alone had the power. Others believe that this was just the most logical place for the provision. Nonetheless, in 1863, Congress passed the Habeas Corpus Act, which gave the president the right to suspend *habeas corpus.* The Great Writ was selectively suspended until 1866.

The suspension of *habeas corpus* is of contemporary concern because the United States recently detained two Americans, Yasser Hamdi and Jose Padilla, as "enemy combatants." Hamdi was eventually released. We are being forced to reconsider civil liberties during times of war and detentions of citizens without due process. The Bush administration's arguments and actions parallel those of Lincoln.

The late Chief Justice Rehnquist, in a 1998 interview, said, "Certainly Lincoln, more so than Franklin Roosevelt, did suppress civil liberties during the Civil War, but both Lincoln and Roosevelt were devoted to—Lincoln to winning the Civil War, saving the union, and Roosevelt to winning World War II. And I think an executive in that position is probably not going to be a great champion of civil liberty."

Despite the fact that suspension of habeas corpus is seen as a "blemish" on Lincoln's record, it hasn't deterred our government from following in his footsteps.

Behaving like a tyrant extended beyond Lincoln to Union army generals who he appointed. General William Tecumseh Sherman was notorious for waging war against innocent civilians. When Confederates targeted Union gunboats on the Mississippi River in Tennessee, Sherman burned an entire town in Tennessee. Observers noted that "small Union units under his command expelled families from river towns and killed others who refused to be evacuated."[20]

Sherman ordered his troops to burn Jackson, Mississippi, even though the Confederate army had already evacuated. Sherman later bragged that "the [civilian] inhabitants are subjugated. They cry aloud for mercy. The land is devastated for 30 miles around . . . we have annihilated the city."[21]

Sherman thought that the large number of civilian deaths was "a beautiful sight" because these would hasten a Union victory. He even boasted about the amount of private property that his troops destroyed during his "march to the sea." He admitted that they stole

$20 million from banks and individuals and demolished at least $100 million in private property.

TAXING TENURE

Abraham Lincoln was committed to taxing Americans to the fullest extent of their tolerance, and he would not let the Constitution stand in his way. During his presidency, the federal government developed a national economic program. This was theretofore unseen in the United States. Notably, Karl Marx himself wrote Lincoln in November 1864: "Sir, We congratulate the American people upon your re-election by a large majority."[22]

Lincoln's tax policies were not in the best interests of a free democratic nation. From 1861 to 1865, duties on imports were increased several times per year. The tax rate on imports was almost 50 percent by 1862. This was said to serve the interests of domestic producers, mainly Northern domestic producers who financed the activities of the Republican Party.

During the war, and under Lincoln's leadership, the first income tax was imposed (the Revenue Act of 1861). Additionally, tax rates on occupational licensing, stamps, and inheritance were also increased. This expanded the reach of the federal government, creating an interface between it and individuals that had not previously existed. National banks were established under the National Currency Acts of 1863 and 1864. They competed with, and bankrupted, many state banks.

With the funds raised through Lincoln's taxation program, the federal government was able to address the debt created by the war, in addition to which it began spending under the General Welfare Clause (much as Roosevelt did in later years). The government diverted war funds to subsidize the construction of railroads in certain parts of the country. It also began dispensing farm welfare. Under Lincoln, Congress enacted the Homestead Act, which gave away federal property.

Under the Homestead Act of 1862, vast amounts of public property were turned over to private citizens. The federal government gave away 270 million acres of land under this act. Anyone who was at least twenty-one years of age could receive a parcel of 160 acres, if he lived on the land and improved it for five years. The Homestead Act encouraged many people to settle in the West, but where was the constitutional authority to do this?

Many of the criticisms that have been leveled against "liberals," New Deal politics, and even against the War on Terror are nothing new. Lincoln's presidency saw all of these issues: economic protectionism, erosion of civil liberties during wartime, and violations of the principle of separation of powers.[23]

Recent studies of Abraham Lincoln have ended the myth of Lincoln as an honest person acting in the best interests of the people. Even though he issued the Emancipation Proclamation, freeing the slaves was only a side effect of defeating the Confederacy.

Lincoln forthrightly declared, "My paramount object in this struggle is to save the Union, and is not either to save or to destroy slavery. If I could save the Union without freeing any slave I would do it, and if I could save it by freeing all the slaves I would do it; and if I could save it by freeing some and leaving others alone I would also do that."[24]

Saying that Lincoln abolished slavery and calling him the "Great Emancipator" are grossly inadequate mischaracterizations. Lincoln was interested in promoting his political agenda of centralizing government power, and freeing the slaves was only a means of the advancement of that end.

Lincoln replaced a voluntary association of states with a strong centralized government. The president and his party eagerly lifted the floodgates to the modern thuggish style of ruling that the U.S. government now employs.

Lincoln increased the power of the federal government at the expense of the rights of the states and civil liberties. This opened the door to more unconstitutional acts by the government in the 1900s through to today. He tried to justify his actions under the guise of public safety. He did not seem to realize that the Founders accounted for war. The Founders thought that the rights enumerated in the Constitution were too important to be abridged. Ever!

The next time you see Lincoln's portrait on a five-dollar bill, remember how many civil liberties he took away from you!

5

THE MANY FACES OF COMMERCE

How Government Signed Its Own Blank Check

After the Civil War ended, as industrialization was changing the nature of the national economy, Congress passed many new federal economic regulations. The Sherman Antitrust Act of 1890 and the Interstate Commerce Act of 1887 inaugurated a new era of federal legislation.

But that legislation ran into a roadblock. Scholars and judges of this period increasingly espoused a belief in laissez faire principles, whereby less government interference in the free markets would make for a better system. Between 1887 and 1937, the Supreme Court championed these principles. The justices ruled that the Constitution, by its recognition of private property, freedom to contract, and due process, dictated that the federal government should not play a role in regulating the economy.

This was in part due to the Court's continued belief in Natural Law principles. Laissez faire philosophy incorporates a belief in the freedom of property, the freedom of contract, and human advancement and prosperity through individual choices and property ownership.

Under Natural Law, the freedom to trade is an important right of all human beings. The Constitution explicitly prohibits the states and by implication the federal government from interfering with private contracts. Under the Fifth Amendment, private property rights are enforceable because the federal government cannot take private property without paying just compensation, and it cannot impair an individual's property or liberty without due process.

This era was not just a significant period in constitutional history because of the Court's philosophy. It was the first time since the Marshall era that we see the aggressive use of judicial review, but this time to uphold the natural rights of individuals by restraining the government from interfering with them.

The Court used its power to further a "dual federalist" form of government where the federal and state governments act as separate sovereigns, each with its own "zone of power." The justices believed their role was to keep the federal government and the states within their respective constitutional boundaries.

During this period, federal laws were repeatedly invalidated in order to limit the scope of federal power and maintain the dual sovereignties required by the Constitution. The Court regularly struck down congressional legislation as exceeding the scope of Congress's commerce power or as violating the Tenth Amendment, or as interfering with basic human freedom as known and understood from Natural Law.

CARVING THE COMMERCE BABY

Federalism was embodied in several important doctrines that the Court implemented to guide its decision-making. The principles represented by these doctrines served to limit the scope of congressional and therefore federal power until the central planners of the New Deal came into power.

First, the Court narrowly defined commerce as "intercourse" in one stage of business, namely *trade*. This was separate from earlier stages such as mining, manufacturing, and production. Congress did not have the power to regulate in those areas that were not under the umbrella of trade because the Constitution only gave it power to regulate interstate commerce.

In the case of *United States v. E.C. Knight* (1895), Congress had attempted to block the American Sugar Refining Company from acquiring four competing refineries. This acquisition would have given American Sugar domination of more than 98 percent of the sugar industry in America. The Court held that the Sherman Antitrust Act could not be used to stop a monopoly in the sugar refining industry because the Constitution does not allow Congress to govern *production* and *manufacturing*. It only permitted Congress to regulate *commerce* or *trade* across state borders.

The second way that the Court limited government power was by requiring that the activity Congress was attempting to regulate must have a *substantial* or *direct effect* on interstate commerce. In *A.L.A. Schecter Poultry Corp. v. United States* (1935), often called the "sick chickens" case, a portion of New Deal legislation called the National Industrial Recovery Act was declared unconstitutional because the trade that Congress had attempted to regulate did not have a sufficient effect on interstate commerce. A key portion of the act gave the president power to govern wages, minimum work ages, and hours of employees.

Pursuant to this law, the president approved a Live Poultry Code for New York City. How would the Founders have felt about the president of the United States regulating chickens in the Big Apple? In the past, the code had been implemented to prevent sellers from requiring buyers to purchase an entire coop of chickens that may have included a sick one. The Court said that because the code concerned only the operations of businesses within New York City, without a "direct effect" on interstate commerce, the federal government did not have regulatory authority.

The Supreme Court declared that maintaining the distinction between "substantial" or direct effects on one hand and "indirect" or minimal effects on commerce on the other hand "must be recognized as . . . essential to the maintenance of our constitutional system."

The justices warned that if Congress were allowed to venture into the regulation of "transactions which could be said to have [only] an indirect effect upon interstate commerce, the federal authority would embrace practically all the activities of the people." Imagine if this Court could see us now!

The Court boldly made clear distinctions between the role of federal and state power in order to protect federalism and the independence of the states. It did this even though it was widely perceived as thumbing its nose at Congress.

In *Railroad Retirement Board v. Alton R.R. Co.* (1935), the Court declared the Railroad Retirement Act of 1934, which forced private companies to spend their profits on pensions for retired railroad workers, unconstitutional. The Court reasoned that Congress could not use its commerce power to require pension programs, because social welfare measures are very different from the movement of goods between merchants across interstate borders.

The Constitutional Convention in 1787 was brought about in large measure by the disorderly state of commerce in the new country. In-state merchants could influence state legislatures to impose taxes and tariffs to protect their own interests and discriminate against goods from merchants in other states by making them more expensive to purchase in-state. Laws governing commerce were often incoherent. The reason for the Commerce Clause was to ensure that regulation of interstate commerce was consistent throughout the states so that commerce could flow freely among them.

Article I, Section 8 of the Constitution directly grants to Congress the power to regulate interstate commerce. Thus, the regulation of interstate commerce is a specific, delegated, enumerated power granted to Congress. It is not clear what the Founders intended by the word "commerce," but today, our definitions of "interstate" and "regulate" differ from what the Founders meant.

The Supreme Court historically used the Commerce Clause to limit the power of the states to interfere with the free flow of commerce. Starting in the twentieth century, though, the Court construed the Commerce Clause more as a source of power for Congress rather than a limitation on the power of the states.

During the 1800s, the Supreme Court frequently decided how extensive states' regulations of commerce could be before they interfered with the authority of Congress. The Constitution limited the regulatory power of the states in favor of the free market.

During this time, the Court believed that it was too much of a stretch to use the Commerce Clause whenever an activity had an indirect effect on commerce. Under the balance of powers set forth in the Constitution, it is up to the Court to restrain the Congress if it exceeds its authority under the Commerce Clause. Up until 1937, the Court pretty much did just that.

In *Carter v. Carter Coal Co.* (1936), the Court declared the Bituminous Coal Conservation Act of 1935 unconstitutional because it extended federal power beyond the boundaries of the Commerce Clause. This act governed practices of the coal industry, including prices, hours, and wages of employees.

"Commerce," said the Court, is distinguished from "production."

Commerce is the *movement* of goods, and that is separate from setting working hours, wages, and employing workers, which are all local activities, regulable—if at all[1]—by the states.

Invalidating the federal law, the Supreme Court through Justice Sutherland wrote that such a narrow construction of the Commerce Clause was essential to protect the independence of the states. In the opinion, the Court warned of starting down the slippery slope toward central planning of the economy in Washington D.C. Justice Sutherland stated for the Court: "Every journey to a forbidden end begins with a first step; and the danger of such a step by the federal government in the direction of taking over the powers of the states is that the end of the journey may find states so despoiled of their powers."

The Court was doing its best to reign in what later became the monstrous power of the federal government over American industry.

COMMERCIAL SUCCESS

Gibbons v. Ogden was the first significant case that explained the Commerce Clause, defined "commerce," and elaborated on its meaning. Chief Justice Marshall wrote the majority opinion and said that commerce was more than "traffic," it was "intercourse." (Talk about words having different meanings today!)

New York first passed legislation limiting the use of the state's ports in 1787 when it granted a man named Fitch the exclusive right to operate passenger steamships in the waterways around New York City. Fitch eventually transferred his monopoly to Fulton and Livingston. Thereafter, no one could operate a steamship around New York City without permission from Fulton and Livingston. At the same time, New Jersey and Connecticut each had their own laws regarding navigation, as did virtually every state. Ogden then acquired the exclusive right to operate steamships in the waters from Fulton and Livingston.

Gibbons was a citizen of New Jersey who began operating a steamship that transported people from Hoboken, New Jersey, to New York City. Ogden saw Gibbons's business as infringing upon Ogden's New York license. Ogden brought a lawsuit against Gibbons in New York.

The case eventually arrived at the Supreme Court, and Gibbons claimed that the New York law giving Ogden an exclusive license was an unconstitutional regulation of interstate commerce by the State of New York because it interfered with the power of Congress to regulate under the Commerce Clause. While Gibbons claimed that his New Jersey license was valid, Ogden claimed that his New York license granted him a monopoly on navigation in and around New York City.

The Supreme Court, addressing how the Commerce Clause should be construed, said commerce is more than just traffic of passengers. Marshall defined commerce as commercial "intercourse." Marshall said, "If commerce does not include navigation, the government of the Union has no direct power over that subject, and can make no law prescribing what shall constitute American vessels, or requiring that they shall be navigated by American seamen. Yet this power has been exercised from the commencement of the government, has been exercised with the consent of all, and has been understood by all to be a commercial regulation." But he also wrote that interstate commerce does not include purely in-state activities. Marshall wrote, "The genius and character of the whole [federal] government seems to be, that its action is to be applied to all the external concerns of the nation, and to those internal concerns which affect the states generally; but not to those which are completely within a particular state, which do not affect other states, and with which it is not necessary to interfere. . . ."

So Congress could regulate intrastate activities which affect interstate commerce and thereby other states. Marshall could not have imagined how far this concept would be extended in violation of the intent of the Founders of the Constitution.

The Court noted that even though Congress can regulate interstate commerce, the states still have the right to regulate commercial activities within their borders. This right extended back to the time before the Constitution was written and was obviously never delegated away. The only check on this power is the Natural Law or the interference with Congress's Commerce Clause power.

Regarding commerce, the powers of the states and the federal government do not overlap. Congress may only regulate interstate commerce, while states may only regulate those activities taking place or having an effect within their borders. If a state law conflicts with a federal law, then under the Supremacy Clause, the federal law will govern. In *Gibbons v. Ogden*, the Court held that the exclusive license granted by New York was invalid. Navigation is clearly commerce, and traveling from New York to New Jersey by steamship is clearly interstate. Therefore, only Congress could regulate this activity.

A few years after *Gibbons v. Ogden* was decided, the Supreme Court heard the case of *Willson v. Black Bird Creek Marsh Company* (1829). In this case, the Court (although ruling in the state's favor in this one instance) articulated the bigger role for Congress under the Commerce Clause in limiting state regulatory power.

Delaware permitted a private company to construct a dam. Once the dam had been built, it blocked a creek, thus blocking commercial traffic. The defendants damaged the dam with their boat and were sued for the cost of repairs.

Arguing that the dam was an impediment to commerce, the

defendants claimed that constructing it should have been prohibited. The defendants argued that the Commerce Clause prevented states from interfering with interstate commerce by closing a previously navigable creek.

Chief Justice Marshall made it clear that a state law could violate the Commerce Clause even if Congress had not passed any laws regulating commerce in the area. This is sometimes called the "dormant" power of the Commerce Clause. However, in *Willson,* the Court held that the commerce power did not apply: Delaware had properly allowed the construction of a dam across a navigable creek, even though it obstructed commerce.

The Court found that Delaware had a valid state interest when it built the dam and that it was within its power to regulate affairs within its borders. Congress had not expressed an intention to keep the creek navigable. Therefore, the Court found that Delaware's action was not a regulation of commerce, but merely managing its own internal affairs.

FIGHT OF THE NAVIGATORS

The sticking point in the case of *Cooley v. Board of Wardens* (1851) was a Philadelphia ordinance requiring that "every ship or vessel arriving from or bound to any foreign port or place, and every ship or vessel of the burden of seventy-five tons or more, sailing from or bound to any port not within the river Delaware, shall be obliged to receive a [local] pilot." Ships that refused to pay a local pilot to guide the ship to port were still obligated to pay half the usual pilot fee. Pilots were common in harbors at the time. It was easy for wooden ships to crash into underwater rocks and then sink. Philadelphia claimed it passed the law to encourage ships entering its harbor to accept a local pilot who knew the harbor well.

Cooley owned and operated two ships subject to this law. He claimed that the Philadelphia law was really written to give work to local pilots and that regulation of pilot fees constituted an unconstitutional regulation of commerce. Congress required all ships engaging in commercial trade to obtain a federal license. Cooley claimed that the federal license gave his ships the ability to engage in interstate commerce unobstructed by local requirements.

The Supreme Court decided against Cooley. It ruled that the pilot requirement was local, only attempted to make the port of Philadelphia a safer place, and only incidentally imposed a regulation on interstate commerce. Justice Curtis noted that even if the law was a regulation of commerce, Congress did not possess the exclusive power to regulate commerce. Because Congress had not passed any laws that conflicted with the local law, the Philadelphia ordinance was valid and did not offend the Commerce Clause.

Gibbons v. Ogden held that "No preference shall be given, by any regulation of commerce or revenue, to the ports of one State over those of another; nor shall vessels to or from one State, be obliged to enter, clear, or pay duties in another." That is the great statement of the law, and it is the singular purpose of the Commerce Clause, to make commerce regular by preventing the states from interfering with it. The Constitution mandated that both Congress and the states can regulate interstate commerce as long as their laws do not conflict.

On balance, Chief Justice Marshall had a tendency to make the federal government bigger and more costly to taxpayers. However, this was tempered by his inclinations to theories of Natural Law. Marshall understood the distinction between interstate commerce, which the Constitution lets the Congress regulate, and intrastate commerce, which only the states, tempered by the free market and Natural Law, can regulate.[2]

For one hundred years after Marshall died, the Supreme Court basically defined commerce as the movement of goods and persons across state borders and did not let Congress widen the definition. The Court safeguarded the Constitution against assaults by Congress. Free enterprise and federalism saw a resurgence that lasted, by and large, until the constitutional monstrosity known as the New Deal.

6

UNFREE TO BIND

The Contract on Contracts

The freedom to contract is an essential Natural Law right. The essence of humanity is the freedom to make choices. Who is the government to tell you the terms of your private dealings?

Article I, Section 10, Clause 1 of the U.S. Constitution contains what is commonly referred to as the Contracts Clause. It states, "No State shall enter into any Treaty, Alliance, or Confederation; grant Letters of Marque and Reprisal; coin Money; emit Bills of Credit; make any Thing but gold and silver Coin a Tender in Payment of Debts; pass any Bill of Attainder, ex post facto Law, or Law impairing the Obligation of Contracts, or grant any Title of Nobility." Under the Contracts Clause, the states are prohibited from interfering with obligations under private contracts. But the Supreme Court has never faithfully interpreted the clause.

In *Home Building & Loan Association v. Blaisdell* (1934), the U.S. Supreme Court held that a Minnesota law prohibiting banks from foreclosing mortgages that were in default did not violate the Contracts Clause.

Despite the majority's approval of this interference with free contracts and undue regulation of commerce, the dissenting justices remained true to the text and spirit of the Constitution, including its prohibition on interference with contracts. In his dissent, Justice Sutherland wrote, "whether the legislation under review is wise or unwise is a matter with which we have nothing to do. Whether it is likely to work well or work ill presents a question entirely irrelevant to the issue. The only legitimate inquiry we can make is whether it is constitutional. If it is not, its virtues, if it has any, cannot save it; if it is, its faults cannot be invoked to accomplish its destruction. *If the provisions of the Constitution be not upheld when they pinch as well as when they comfort, they may as well be abandoned.*"[1]

Justice Sutherland wrote that the "effect of the Minnesota legislation, though serious enough in itself, is of trivial significance compared with the far more serious and dangerous inroads upon the limitations of the Constitution."

Mr. and Mrs. John H. Blaisdell had borrowed money from Home Building & Loan to buy a house. As security for the loan, they gave a mortgage on the house to the bank. The mortgage said that if they defaulted on the loan, the bank could foreclose on the house, sell it, pay itself back the unpaid loan, and remit the remainder to the Blaisdells. This was a standard, freely negotiated contract. But the State of Minnesota, believing its legislators and bureaucrats knew how to protect the Blaisdells from their own agreements, and happy to help a bank, its investors, and depositors lose money, enacted legislation instituting a moratorium on foreclosures. Justice Sutherland referred to a decision written by Chief Justice Taney when he said, "while the Constitution remains unaltered, it must be construed now as it was understood at the time of its adoption."

Cue the flashback. In 1785, before the Constitution came into being, the Charles River Bridge Company entered into a contract with the State of Massachusetts to build a bridge across the Charles River, so as to connect Boston to Cambridge. In return for building the bridge, Massachusetts agreed that the company could collect tolls from travelers and the State would not permit another bridge to be built across the Charles River. In 1828, the Massachusetts legislature allowed the Warren Bridge Company to build another bridge across the Charles River close to the original one. Its bridge did not charge a toll. The new free bridge resulted in a reduction of traffic and tolls on the old bridge, so the Charles River Bridge Company sued, alleging that the subsequent legislature had interfered with Charles River Company's contract with the earlier legislature.

The issue in *River Bridge v. Warren Bridge* (1837) was whether the Massachusetts legislature's agreement with the Charles River Bridge Company was a contract. If it was, the Contracts Clause was violated, as the contract with Warren Bridge violated the terms of the contract with Charles River Company, and the violator was the State of Massachusetts, as the Contracts Clause prohibits the states from interfering with contracts, even those to which they are a party.

To limit the circumstances in which government charters could be viewed as contracts, the Supreme Court did something that would have made George Orwell blush. It held that the agreement between Charles River Company and the State of Massachusetts, the one for which they each freely negotiated, the one which outlawed the subsequent building of another bridge on the river, the one in which the Charles River Company spent its own money to build a bridge in return for an agreement that no other bridges would be built there, was not a contract!

The Court ruled that the legislature did not give exclusive control over the waters by chartering the bridge. The justices declared that the economic interests of the local area trumped private property rights, even though these rights are explicitly protected by the U.S. Constitution.

Four years earlier, in *Bronson v. Kinzie* (1843), the U.S. Supreme

Court had heard a case originating with a dispute over the payment of a mortgage. The real issue in the case was the action of the Illinois Legislature that interfered with the private mortgage contract. When Kinzie defaulted, Bronson filed a lawsuit to foreclose the mortgage. However, after the mortgage had been made but before the lawsuit was filed, the Illinois legislature passed a law affecting the rights of mortgage holders. The Court had to decide whether the Illinois law violated the Contracts Clause by interfering with the obligations of the parties under their private mortgage contract.

It ruled that the law of Illinois at the time the mortgage was entered into was relevant, and any subsequent state legislation was to be ignored in determining rights and remedies under the contract. The Supreme Court held that a state cannot materially impair the *duties* of private parties under a contract. A state legislature can modify the *remedies* available under a contract, though. For example, the Court held that a legislature may shorten the statute of limitations for a duty owed under a contract. Or a state may specify the remedies available in the event of a breach of contact.

Even more drastically, in *Stone v. Mississippi* (1890), the Supreme Court suggested that it would allow a state to interfere with a private contract in violation of the Contracts Clause if the state did so under its police power. Imagine the Supreme Court turning a blind eye to the Constitution and the Contracts Clause just because a state claims it has a "valid police purpose" for interfering with a contract! Sadly, this was not far off. This principle was later expanded to allow state activities that were nothing more than the redistribution of wealth.

YOU BET YOUR RIGHTS!

In 1867, the Mississippi legislature chartered a society to operate lotteries for the next quarter century. One year later, it enacted a law that prohibited lotteries in the state!

In 1874, the police raided the society, and John Stone was among those arrested. The State of Mississippi said that the license was invalid due to the new legislation. The issue here was whether Mississippi violated the Contracts Clause in the Constitution by repealing its grant to the society. Unanimously, the justices ruled that outlawing lotteries was constitutional, regardless of what was stated in the charter that Mississippi gave to the lottery society, and regardless of what is stated in the Constitution.

The Court ruled that state legislatures cannot validly compel future generations to follow their decisions and "bargain away public health and morals." Even if the legislature votes a certain way, future generations can overturn the existing rules with new legislation. The right to engage in things that the Court considered immoral, such as lotteries, was governed by contract. The legislature can validly change the contract rights of private citizens. This is, of course, purely Positivist thought that violates the Natural Law right of people to enter into their own contracts and to be bound by them.

As we saw earlier, a "taking" by definition is an action by the government that decreases the value of private property. When the State of Mississippi rescinded the right to hold lotteries, it took a valuable right away from private persons. If the state legislature was concerned about holding lotteries, then it should not have entered into a long-term contract that allowed them. When the Massachusetts government built a free bridge near the toll bridge, it did not directly take private property. However, its actions indirectly affected the value of the toll bridge.

In both the lottery and bridge cases, the state government, as well as interfering with contracts, took away the rights of private persons (the shareholders of the corporations) without providing just compensation. These are blatant violations of the Takings Clause. Even if physical property is not directly confiscated, a loss of the benefit of a bargain is still a taking. The government should provide fair compensation whenever it takes profitable contract rights away from private individuals.

Unfortunately, the Court opened the door to a vast array of state government regulations that trampled on contractual rights. Any state legislation enacted for the "public good" or the "public safety" would then justify the impairment of, or interference with, contractual duties.

BACK TO BLAISDELL

All of this set the stage for the Supreme Court's decision in *Blaisdell.* It is an unforgivable assault on the Natural Law right to contract. When the Court upheld the Minnesota law that prevented mortgage holders from foreclosing on mortgages for a two-year period, its ruling sanctioned precisely the sort of legislation that the Contracts Clause was written to prevent. What is the value of a binding contract if, when it stings one of the parties, the state comes to the rescue?

In this case, the Court flatly subordinated the Contracts Clause to whatever the Court and a state legislature would deem a "valid police purpose"! It also dismissed the Founders' intent for the Contracts Clause as irrelevant. Chief Justice Hughes wrote, "It is no answer . . . to insist that what the provision of the Constitution meant to the vision of that day, it must mean to the vision of our time. If by the statement that what the Constitution meant at the time of its adoption it means today, it is intended to say that the great clauses of the Constitution must be confined to the interpretation which the Founders, with the conditions and outlook of their time would have placed upon them, the statement carries its own refutation."

This is the strongest statement of this kind ever made in constitutional history. *The Court explicitly held that the Founders' intent is irrelevant in the interpretation of constitutional language,* and thus the meaning of the fundamental law of the land changes with each generation. If the above language were to be controlling in all constitutional interpretation, then the Constitution could be interpreted to mean anything that serves present day convenience.

The Court also stressed that the law "was not for the mere advantage of particular individuals but for the protection of a basic interest in society," meaning that it is to serve a greater societal good, rather than protect the freedom of the individual from the abuses of government.

Wrong.

The Constitution was intended to protect individuals and minorities from the tyranny of a more numerous and powerful majority.

The dissent of Justice Sutherland has become a mantra for all who believe in limited government. "If the provisions of the Constitution be not upheld when they pinch as well as when they comfort, they may as well be abandoned."

Blaisdell is extremely significant in that it marks the clear turning point away from the Court's laissez faire, free market philosophy, as well as a repudiation of the Contracts Clause. The Court was no longer concerned with keeping the markets open and free. It was no longer concerned with keeping the government small. It was no longer concerned with enforcing freely consented-to agreements. Its new priority was "the common good," and making sure that the government would provide for it.

Justice Antonin Scalia once cautioned, "If the courts are free to write the Constitution anew, they will, by God, write it the way the majority wants; the appointment and confirmation process will see to that. This, of course, is the end of the Bill of Rights, whose meaning will be committed to the very body it was meant to protect us against: *the majority.*"

CONTRACT OUT

In *Allgeyer v. Louisiana* (1897), the Court invalidated a Louisiana law that prohibited residents from purchasing property insurance from out-of-state sellers. The case revealed the Court's willingness to apply the due process doctrine to strike down any economic or social legislation that unreasonably infringed on an individual's natural right to enter into a binding contract.

Essentially, if individuals or groups or corporations are not given a fair opportunity to be heard or adequate representation when a decision is made affecting their rights, then they are considered to have been denied due process. Denial of due process is prohibited by the Fifth and Fourteenth Amendments and will frequently result in a law being overturned.

Yet, in October 1894, the State of Louisiana enacted a law to prevent individuals and corporations from entering into business deals with maritime insurance companies who had not been licensed to do business within the State. Under the law, persons or entities who contracted with out-of-state insurers to insure property within the State would be subject to a fine of one thousand dollars per offense.

The defendant, E. Allgeyer & Co., was in the business of exporting cotton from Louisiana to Great Britain and continental Europe. Allgeyer sought $3,400 worth of insurance for a hundred bales of cotton that were to be shipped to foreign ports by sending a "letter of advice or certificate of marine insurance" from New Orleans to the Atlantic Mutual Insurance Company of New York. Atlantic Mutual was a New York maritime insurance company that did not have an agent in Louisiana and had not complied with the statutory requirements to do business in Louisiana.

This case was not about whether or not Atlantic Mutual was

doing business illegally in Louisiana. The lawyers for Louisiana did not make that contention. Because Atlantic Mutual was not certified to operate in the state of Louisiana, the agreement with Allgeyer was considered to have been made in New York, where Atlantic was located, and the contract between it and Allgeyer was deemed a New York contract. Thus, the government of Louisiana contended that because of its law, Allgeyer was not free to make that contract.

The contract itself provided that it was legal in New York and was a valid contract. It was drafted outside of the state in order to be executed outside of Louisiana. Thus the validity of the contract was also not at issue here. The Court characterized the correspondence between Allgeyer and Atlantic Mutual as "a mere notification that the contract already in existence would attach to that particular property." The question regards the behavior of the parties. The prohibited conduct was the "act of writing within [Louisiana], the letter of notification. . . ."

The Court said that the statute, by forbidding the performance of a valid contract made out of state, violates the due process guarantee contained in the Fourteenth Amendment of the Constitution. Freedom of contract does not require a state to permit any and every business to operate within its borders. Justice Peckham conceded in his opinion that a state reserves the right to exclude businesses from operating in its jurisdiction. However, the state cannot abridge the rights of in-state person to contract for services outside of the state.

LEGENDARY LOCHNER

In 1897, the New York legislature passed an act, as part of its labor law, containing a provision regarding bakeries, which stated that "no employee shall be required or permitted to work in a biscuit, cake, or bread bakery or confectionary establishment" for more than ten hours per day. The Supreme Court later characterized the act as "an absolute prohibition upon the employer, permitting, under any circumstances, more than ten hours work to be done in his establishment."

Joseph Lochner was the owner of a bakery in Utica, New York, and was indicted for allowing an employee to work more than sixty hours in a one-week period. This was his second offense under the act. New York attempted to justify the law under its police power, that is, as a measure enacted to protect the health, safety, welfare, or morality of those within its borders.

One might ask from where the State of New York derived the right to take proactive measures to protect an individual from voluntary "overwork." New York claimed that its interest in having good, healthy workers gave it the right to safeguard its bakers. As evidence of its concern, New York cited the wording of the statute, i.e., that an employee could neither be permitted nor required to work more than ten hours, as an attempt to protect the employee from "his own lack of knowledge."

The Court, however, noted that this wording made that act an "absolute prohibition upon the employer." It was mandatory and contained no provision for emergencies, such as an employee's need to earn extra money or a staff shortage requiring an employee to work overtime.

The Supreme Court first invoked not the Contracts Clause but the Fourteenth Amendment to invalidate that statute, just as it had in *Allgeyer*. The Court held that the act "necessarily interfered with the right of contract between the employer and employees." As it had in *Allgeyer*, the Court reasoned that the right to make a contract "is part of the liberty of the individual protected by the Fourteenth Amendment of the Federal Constitution."

Justice Peckham then concluded that the right to "purchase or sell labor" was also protected under the liberty provision of the Fourteenth Amendment. That means it cannot be taken away by the legislature but only by a jury after procedural due process.

According to the Court, the State's police power would grant the state the right to interfere with certain types of contracts. In reviewing the police power precedent, the Court acknowledged that some types of work have been legitimate objects of the State's police power because of the nature of the work involved. It cited as examples highly dangerous work, such as miners, coal workers, and smelters.

In these cases, the law did make exceptions for emergencies (where life or property were endangered). The Court also noted that the peculiar conditions affecting people who worked in underground mines made them an appropriate target for exercise of the police power by allowing the states to compel safety measures in the mines. Additionally, the Court noted that these workers were in some cases held to be disadvantaged.

In terms of safety and welfare, the Court concluded, "There is no contention that bakers as a class are not equal in intelligence and capacity to men in other trades or manual occupations, or that they are not able to assert their rights and care for themselves without the protecting arm of the State, interfering with their independence of judgment and of action."

However, if there were a genuine health issue present, the Court would have upheld the law as a proper regulation of police power subject to some qualifications. In the *Lochner* case, there was no genuine health issue.

The wonderful opinion states, "It is a question of which of two powers or rights shall prevail—the power of the State to legislate or the right of the individual to liberty of person and freedom of contract. . . . The act must have a more direct relation, as a means to an end, and the end itself must be appropriate and legitimate, before an act can be held to be valid which interferes with the general right of an individual to be free in his person and in his power to contract in relation to his own labor."

The Court suggested that the freedom to contract is so fundamental that even if there were evidence that employment as a baker was somewhat unhealthy, solid proof of extreme unhealthiness would have to be met for the police power to trump the freedom to contract: "We think that there can be no fair doubt that the trade of a baker, in and of itself, is not an unhealthy one *to that degree* which would authorize the legislature to interfere with the right to labor" (emphasis added). As far as statistics demonstrating the relative health of the profession, the Court said, "it may be true that the trade of a baker does not appear to be as healthy as some other trades, and is also vastly more healthy than still others."

Concerned with starting down a slippery slope, where no industry would be safe from regulation because of potential health risks, the Court invalidated the State's claimed right as supervisor, or *pater familias,* which interferes with individual liberties, the Contracts Clause, and the Due Process Clauses. How can the State determine the amount of work that constitutes overwork or will raise a health concern? Why cannot an individual make that determination for himself?

Justice Peckham had little regard for state intrusion into industry regulation in general. "Statutes of the nature of that under review, limiting the hours in which grown and intelligent men may labor to earn their living, are mere meddlesome interferences with the rights of the individual," he wrote.

Justice Peckham understood that the Contracts Clause was put into the Constitution to protect the inherent right of persons to choose to enter into private contracts without worrying about government intervention. If people know that the government will nullify any subsequently objectionable contracts that they enter into, then their choices will always be subject to the government's approval.

Contracts will become meaningless if their obligations cannot be enforced. Then freedom suffers because the free choice to enter into the agreement becomes meaningless.

7

RESTRAINING CONGRESS

As we have seen, there existed a period of time when what was written in the Constitution was zealously protected by the judicial branch. The Court had the utmost respect for the restraints that the "tortured document" imposed on Congress. For the first hundred years of our nation's history following the death of John Marshall, the Court usually interpreted the Constitution to mean what it said. The Supreme Court protected economic liberties such as freedom of contract, freedom to pursue a livelihood, and freedom to practice a trade or a profession from interference by the states.

With the notable exceptions of the creation of a central bank, Lincoln's naïve economic shenanigans, Teddy Roosevelt's central planning, and Woodrow Wilson's suppression of civil liberties during World War I, Congress, the president, and the Supreme Court respected the Constitution and their respective roles under it. The great constitutional crises before the New Deal era were fomented by the states. But from time to time, the Supreme Court restrained the Congress and the president as well as the states from unconstitutional behavior.

It did so rightly. It did so proudly. It did so often. Unfortunately, it rarely did so after this period. It's a depressing story, but there is another story that I love to tell, of the glory days of constitutional respect and protection, of the so-called "Lochner Era" and how we got there.

DON'T SLAUGHTER OUR RIGHTS!

In 1869, amidst the ruins of the Civil War, the Louisiana legislature passed a law that gave a group of seventeen people the sole right to manage a slaughterhouse in the city of New Orleans. Imagine the audacity of this group of politicians! In an era without refrigeration, when meat was consumed soon after purchase, every slaughterhouse except one had to shut down. Anyone who wanted to be a butcher could only work at that one slaughterhouse. Butchers were even charged fees for using this facility. It was a clear power grab by a bunch of corrupt, central planning Positivists in the legislature.

Twenty-five butchers, barred from their own livelihoods, brought suit in order to invalidate the law under the recently adopted Thirteenth and Fourteenth Amendments of the Constitution. The case went to the U.S. Supreme Court. For centuries, governments in the United States and Europe believed they could validly create monopolies. That didn't stop the butchers who alleged that monopolies were unconstitutional under the Thirteenth Amendment, which abolished slavery. Lawyers argued that the law was a form of involuntary servitude.

Representing the butchers was John A. Campbell, generally recognized as the best lawyer in the South and a former justice of the Supreme Court who had resigned to show his allegiance to the Confederacy. Campbell's eloquent appeal sought to convince the Court that this country had strayed from the intent of the Founders. "What did the colonists and their posterity seek for and obtain by their settlement of this continent? *Freedom, free action, free enterprise—free competition.* It was in freedom they expected to find the best of auspices for every kind of human success. . . ." He claimed that his clients were robbed of their property rights, which violated the Privileges or Immunities Clause of the Constitution. Additionally, the butchers were denied their "due process" and "equal protection" under the Fourteenth Amendment.

The Fourteenth Amendment states, "All persons born or naturalized in the United States and subject to the jurisdiction thereof, are citizens of the United States and of the State wherein they reside. No State shall make or enforce any law which shall abridge the privileges or immunities of citizens of the United States; nor shall any State deprive any person of life, liberty, or property, without due process of law; nor deny to any person within its jurisdiction the equal protection of the laws."

Incredibly, the Court upheld the slaughterhouse monopoly! Justice Samuel F. Miller and a majority of the Court allowed states to grant monopolies under their police power. These "police powers" were vaguely defined by the Court as the authority to pass laws concerning the "safety, health, morals, and general welfare" of the persons in the states.

Does it seem like the Court was being a bit paternalistic? Does it seem like instead of strictly reading the Constitution, the justices were "projecting" (as a psychologist would say) their own personal views of the way things ought to be onto the rest of us?

The Court declared that slavery was outlawed under the Thirteenth Amendment, but laws prohibiting certain business activities were valid. To me, this reasoning is clearly Positive law theory, and against Natural Law—and therefore against the United States Constitution. These five justices also denied that the Fourteenth Amendment's Privileges or Immunities Clause, the Due Process

Clause, and "equal protection" guarantees applied to the right to operate slaughterhouses.

The right to practice your lawful trade seems intuitively a bedrock of human liberty, and a *privilege or immunity* of personhood, the denial of which to some and the protection of which to others would surely be a denial of *equal protection* under law. Nevertheless, the Court refused to elevate these rights to those deserving of constitutional protection and decided that the restraints placed by the Louisiana legislators on the slaughterhouse operators, namely the inability to practice their trade, did not deprive them of their property without due process.

Of course, this denial occurred without any due process. These butchers did not lose a trial before a jury of their peers at which they were convicted of a crime. They lost a vote among politicians in the legislature. It was the legislature that stole their right to work from them.

Under the due process arguments, the Court held the only due process requirement mandated by the Fourteenth Amendment was that of procedural due process (notice of the law, a fair trial before a neutral judge and jury, a loyal lawyer, the right to appeal, etc.), not substantive due process, which has to do with fairness and holds that some fundamental rights can never be validly taken from persons by the legislative or executive branches.

The Court held that the Fourteenth Amendment was only intended to ensure that former slaves had certain freedoms. The Court said its scope as originally planned did not include the right to work.

This case has never been overruled, and has been cited hundreds of times for the principle that the right to work is not fundamental and therefore is not protected by the Constitution.

However, it is not just the majority decision that has gained a legacy over time. Even though the dissenting justices lost, their principles lived on for a significant span of our constitutional history. Their view soon became the view of the majority of the justices of the Supreme Court.

SEND IN THE OPPOSITION!

The *Slaughterhouse* dissenters maintained that the right to work is natural and inalienable and the privileges or immunities clause of the Fourteenth Amendment requires that it not be limited to a favored few. They also argued that the Fourteenth Amendment has requirements of substantive as well as procedural due process.

One of the dissenters, Justice Stephen Field, said, "The immortal document which proclaimed the independence of the country declared as self-evident truths that the Creator had endowed men 'with certain inalienable rights.'" He wrote that the right to work was a natural right, and therefore the Constitution protected it.

Justice Field even referred to Adam Smith's *Wealth of Nations*: "The property which every man has in his own labor, as it is the original foundation of all other property, so it is the most sacred and inviolable. The patrimony of the poor man lies in the strength and dexterity of his own hands; and to hinder him from employing this strength and dexterity in what manner he thinks proper, without injury to his neighbor, is a plain violation of this most sacred property."

Justice Bradley, who also dissented, reiterated: "In my view, a law which prohibits a large class of citizens from adopting a lawful employment, or from following a lawful employment previously adopted, does deprive them of liberty as well as property, without due process of law. Their right of choice is a portion of their liberty; their occupation is their property."

This concept is embodied in chapter seven's discussion on the doctrine of *liberty of contract,* which stands for the premise that the government cannot interfere with private contracts. The dissenters launched the idea of "substantive due process" and "liberty of contract."

THE LOCHNER ERA

Rooted in a Natural Law mind-set, the Supreme Court clearly viewed the protection of the freedom to contract as a God-given right. So much so that the *Lochner* case, in which the Court fully articulated the 1905 doctrine of liberty of contract (which was introduced in chapter six) came to define the time.

In *Lochner*, the Supreme Court declared unconstitutional a New York State law that limited the number of hours a baker could work. How dare a state in the land of opportunity try to steal the liberty of a laborer to work and a small businessperson to employ him? That is precisely what the New York legislature attempted. And this theft is precisely what goes on everyday in twenty-first century America. But the *Lochner* court, one hundred years ago, would have none of it!

The Court held that the "state had no reasonable ground for interfering with liberty by determining the hours of labor for individuals who are free to work as they choose." It found that the law interfered with freedom of contract, it did not serve a valid police power, and it thus violated the Fourteenth Amendment's Due Process Clause because it took away property (the fruits of the agreement) without a trial.

Firmly, the Court established that the "freedom, or liberty of contract was a basic, fundamental right protected by the liberty and property provisions of the Due Process Clause of the Fifth and Fourteenth Amendment." As a natural right, freedom of contract received the greatest judicial protection by the Constitution.

From *Lochner* on, the Court continued to protect natural economic liberties, such as freedom of contract, freedom to pursue a livelihood, and freedom to practice a trade or a profession, using the Due Process Clause of the Fourteenth Amendment.

The Natural Law opinion in *Lochner* boldly shouts, "the general right to make a contract in relation to his business is part of the liberty of the individual protected by the Fourteenth Amendment of the Federal Constitution. Under that provision no state can deprive any person of life, liberty, or property without due process of law. The right to purchase or to sell labor is part of the liberty protected by this amendment." Simply put, the legislative and executive branches of any state or the federal government may not deprive one of life, liberty, or property.

The judiciary's duty is to scrutinize carefully the constitutionality of all legislation to decide if the government that enacted it had the power to do so, and to determine if the legislation violates the Natural Law. The *Lochner* court held that legislation is constitutional if it does not interfere with the freedom of contract and it serves a "legitimate police purpose."

The phrase "legitimate police purpose," referred to "those powers that relate to safety, health, morals, and the general welfare of the public." With great foresight, the justices cautioned that laws purporting to be such exercises of "valid police powers" were typically just shielded attempts to redistribute wealth by regulating the labor or the hours of one group at that group's expense or at the expense of another group.

The intrusive, suffocating law struck down in *Lochner* prevented bakery owners and bakers from contracting for as many hours of work as they wished. Thus the law interfered with the bakers' freedom of contract. This paternalism robbed them of "their independence of judgment and of action." What could be worse than a country where the government tells you that you can live your dreams if you work "hard" enough, but does not allow you to work as "hard" as you choose?

Why stop at bakers in New York? If the law were to stand, then clearly we would be (and indeed were) heading down the slippery slope of regulating the hours of everyone. Who does not need to be regulated as a mechanism to preserve their health? Lawyers? Physicians? Athletes? Judges? Presidents?

Justice Peckham opined, "the act is not, within any fair meaning of the term, a health law, but is an illegal interference with the rights of individuals, both employers and employees, to make contracts regarding labor upon such terms as they may think best, or which they may agree upon with the other parties to such contracts." He hit the nail on the head: who is the government to treat me like a child that needs to be told to stop "playing" and "to go to bed"? And certainly, these "watching out for you" regulations are not rules in a game. They are restrictions on one's livelihood. When the government is acting like an overprotective parent, it forces dependence upon itself.

Politicians create laws under the guise of "helping people" in order to ensure that they have a dependent group of people to continue to vote for them. One of the cruelest things that one can do is to take perfectly capable people and brainwash them to believe that they are not capable.

In the *Lochner* opinion, Justice Peckham explains this view, noting, "statutes of the nature of that under review, limiting the hours in which grown and intelligent men may labor to earn their living, are mere meddlesome interferences with the rights of the individual, and they are not saved from condemnation by the claim that they are passed in the exercise of a police power. . . ."

What a fabulous enunciation of Natural Law principles! We may have abandoned such self-evident truths that the *Lochner* Court reminded us of so eloquently, but it remains one of the most important and frequently cited cases in Supreme Court history. It serves as the yard marker in the ideological battles between the free market Natural Law originalists and the New Deal regulatory state Positivists.

"GLORY DAYS, WELL, THEY'LL PASS YOU BY"

I guess Bruce Springsteen's famous lyric even applies to constitutional interpretation. For the three decades following the 1905 *Lochner* decision, almost two hundred state laws that regulated prices, labor, and maximum or minimum hours were declared unconstitutional as violating the Due Process Clause of the Fourteenth Amendment.

The legal doctrine whereby the liberty of contract—freedom of choice—is protected by the Fourteenth Amendment's Due Process Clause is called "Substantive Due Process." "Substantive" means that the Fourteenth Amendment safeguards more than one's procedural rights to due process under the law, and that any government's attempt to legislate away one's natural rights to life, liberty, and the pursuit of happiness is strictly prohibited. Put another way, life, liberty, and the pursuit of happiness (standing on their own) are themselves protected, not just the means or procedure that the government must use if it wants to take them away.

During the *Lochner* era, these doctrines were the Court's principal source of defense guarding individual rights against governmental encroachment.

BLOCKING SOCIALISM

All through the *Lochner* era, laws purporting to regulate the way in which people labored were struck down, like one blocked field-goal attempt after another. Deeming them interferences with the liberty of contract and violations of substantive due process, the Court kept the do-gooders and wealth redistributors in Congress and state legislatures from stepping on the average guy's toes. The Court did its constitutional duty and kept the grabby legislators in line.

In *Adams v. Tanner* (1917), the Supreme Court struck down a state law that prevented privately owned employment agencies from assessing fees for their services. Why on earth could a private company not be able to profit from its work? Is this the America boatloads of people risked their lives to get to? The Supreme Court would have none of such nonsense.

A few years later, during the height of the Roaring Twenties, in *Jay Burns Baking Co. v. Bryan* (1924), the Court struck down a law requiring standardized weights for bread loaves. Today, that law is reminiscent of the toilet clogging 1992 Energy Policy Act.

Later in the twenties, in *Weaver v. Palmer Bros.* (1926), the Court did the same thing with a Pennsylvania law regulating the use of "shoddy," a material consisting of rags and debris, used in mattresses.

Now, how could anyone in his or her right mind be against keeping rags and debris out of our beds? Well, I cannot imagine anyone who wants to sleep on filth, but I can tell you the Founders would not tell you that you could not sleep on debris if you wanted to do so. With certainty, I can also tell you that the Founders would not want the government in your bedroom; and it certainly is there.

The Founders, you see, gave individuals more credit. Buyers could make up their own mind on what they wanted in their mattresses: rags, feathers, or money. Certainly, though, it was the consumer's right to purchase what he wanted and the companies' right to try to sell what they wanted. Their business was no business for the government.

In 1932, in the case of *New York Ice Co. v. Liebmann*, the Court held that a New York law that required a government permit for any person to manufacture ice was unconstitutional. The Court wrote that the "regulation had the effect of denying or unreasonably curtailing the common right to engage in a lawful business."

By requiring a permit for something as obscure as ice manufacturing, this law created a barrier to entry into this occupation, and by legislating away the freedom to do this work, it violated substantive due process. Without a doubt, the Supreme Court continued to do its job by protecting the natural rights of persons to choose their lines of work and to work as they wished.

TWO CHEERS FOR CHILD LABOR

The Court's commitment to libertarian free market values concerned the limits of Congress's taxing and spending powers as well. In 1919, Congress passed the Child Labor Tax Law, which mandated that all companies that hired children under age fourteen pay a punitive tax on their earnings. Drexel Furniture Company violated the law and was required to pay over $6,000 in taxes, which it challenged in court.

Drexel argued that the act attempted to regulate child labor, which is a state power under the Constitution. However, the federal government claimed that the Congress was exercising its power under the Commerce Clause. Sticking to its strict reading of the Constitution (a foreign idea to many of today's judges and lawmakers), the Supreme Court in *Bailey v. Drexel Furniture Company* (1922) held that the Child Labor Tax Law was unconstitutional because it prevented the states from putting child labor laws into effect.

Chief Justice Taft wrote for the Court that this tax code

overstepped Congress's boundaries and did more than impose an "incidental restraint." Rather, it had a "prohibitory and regulatory effect" in an area where Congress was constitutionally powerless. The Court stated, "although Congress does have power to tax, there is a difference between taxing and punishing." Because the tax had to be paid only by employers who chose not to comply with the age and hours regulations under the act, it was coercive and thus punitive. Clearly, the tax was a form of legislative punishment.

A rightly disgusted Chief Justice Taft knew that this was an imposition on states' rights and "all constitutional limitation of the powers of Congress" under the guise of taxes. "To give such magic to the word 'tax' would be to break down all constitutional limitation of the powers of Congress and completely wipe out the sovereignty of the States." How dare Congress attempt to impose penalties under the guise of taxes?

Continuing its habit of scolding the Congress, the Court found the 1933 Agricultural Adjustment Act unconstitutional. That law created a tax on farm goods, which was a pure redistribution of wealth. The funds would be given to farmers who agreed to plant fewer crops. The Supreme Court held that the act violated the Tenth Amendment by usurping the power of the states to regulate agriculture. Justice Roberts reasoned that although Congress could tax and spend, here that power was "but means to an unconstitutional end," the federal regulation of agriculture.

SEXISM REJECTED

Despite all the great successes of strict interpretation of the Constitution that preceded it, the most memorable tale occurred in 1918. The Nineteenth Amendment had just been passed, giving women the right to vote. Outrageously, the clearly sexist and paternalistic Congress made the argument that without a minimum wage, women would be forced to earn money in an immoral manner. Imagine, women have finally been given the right to express themselves politically, which they were wrongly denied for over a century and a half in America, but they still needed the male Congress to chaperone them.

Congress enacted a law that guaranteed a minimum wage to women and children employed in the District of Columbia. In *Adkins v. Children's Hospital* (1923), the Supreme Court ruled that such a law interfered with the ability of companies and their workers to contract with each other.

In a controversial and progressive move, the Court rejected this argument, and the law was struck down as a violation of the Constitution. The opinion read: "The ancient inequality of the sexes, otherwise than physical, has continued, 'with diminishing intensity.' In view of the great—not to say revolutionary—changes which have taken place since that utterance, in the contractual, political, and civil status of women, culminating in the Nineteenth Amendment, it is not unreasonable to say that these differences have now come almost, if not quite, to the vanishing point. . . . We cannot accept the doctrine that women of mature age . . . require or may be subjected to restrictions upon their liberty of contract, which could not lawfully be imposed in the case of men under similar circumstances."

The Court went on to hold a New York minimum-wage law for women unconstitutional as a violation of substantive due process (the rights of employers and women to agree on a salary). The Court clarified that the rights of companies and workers to contract "is part of the liberty protected by the due process clause." Therefore, the law impermissibly interfered with the freedom of contract, as it did not serve a valid police purpose.

During the *Lochner* era, the Court used the substantive due process doctrine as well as the Commerce Clause as protective shields over freedom's guarantees. Which method the Court employed depended on which government actor was doing the infringing. If a *state* adopted a minimum wage law it would have been struck down as violating the Due Process Clause of the Fourteenth Amendment. However, if it were the *federal government* that attempted to adopt such a law, it was invalidated as exceeding the power given to Congress by the Commerce Clause.

Both were a means to an end. The Supreme Court zealously promoted capitalism, free enterprise, property rights, and freedom to contract from overreaching government regulations.

The justices believed these regulations violated individual natural rights and the Constitution, and were nothing short of paternalistic means to increase government power for the sake of redistributing wealth. And during this period of American history there occurred the most remarkable industrial revolution—indeed the greatest economic growth—the country had ever seen, unaccompanied by increased taxes and bigger government.

THE LONG LOST TENTH AMENDMENT

The third doctrine the Court relied on to advance federalism and protect individual rights was embodied in the Tenth Amendment. The Tenth Amendment has tragically become almost a nullity at the present point in our history. However, as we have seen, during this unique period, the Supreme Court was still interested in reading and applying the Constitution in its entirety.

The constitutional language is clear and concise: "The powers not delegated to the United States by the Constitution, nor prohibited by it to the states, are reserved to the states respectively, or to the people."

The Tenth Amendment reserved a zone of activity to the states that Congress could not regulate. The Court understood that zone of activity to mean control of the police power in public and in the workplace, so federal laws regulating commerce in those spheres were struck down as unconstitutional.

The case of *Hammer v. Dagenhart* (1918) was the most important decision illustrating the protections of the Tenth Amendment. Congress enacted the Keating-Owen Child Labor Act, which halted the shipment of products in interstate commerce taken out of mines or manufactured in factories where children were employed. The father of Reuben Dagenhart brought a lawsuit to protect the freedom of his son, who was only fourteen, to work in a textile mill.

The Court found that Congress had exceeded the bounds of the Commerce Clause because it sought to regulate the conditions of production, not commerce, and that this area of human endeavor was reserved, under the Tenth Amendment, to the states; reserved, because it had never been delegated to the federal government.

The act did not regulate the *transportation* of goods, but rather sought *to standardize the ages and times of the children's employment,* and that standardization is neither contemplated nor authorized by the Commerce Clause. The Court held that the scheme of the act was an unreasonable interference with the free market system. This was so because Congress is without power to equalize market conditions that are not a part of interstate commerce.

The Court acknowledged that it had earlier validated prohibitions of activities in commerce, but only regarding Congress acting within one of the powers delegated to it by the Constitution. "There should be limitations upon the right to employ children in mines and factories in their own interest and in the interest of the public welfare all will admit, and it may be desirable that such laws be uniform, but our Federal Government is one of *enumerated powers* . . ."

The Court went on to state in ominous terms, "The control by Congress over interstate commerce cannot authorize the exercise of authority not entrusted to it by the Constitution. The maintenance of authority of the states over matters purely local is as essential to the preservation of our institutions as is the conservation of the supremacy of the federal power in all matters entrusted to the Nation by the Federal Constitution. . . ."

Even at a more basic level, we must remember that the Founders envisioned a loose confederation of states. They firmly believed in the idea that states should remain potent in governing themselves. Why were they so adamant about this idea? The answer lies in the fact that they had just escaped the tyranny of a king who thought he knew best how to govern local colonies from across an ocean.

The Founders knew two things in this regard. First, proximity is power. Governments and political leaders are best held accountable to the will of the people when government is local. Second, the people of a state know what is best for them; they do not need bureaucrats, miles away in Washington D.C., governing their lives.

Substantive due process, liberty of contract, and the Tenth Amendment fascinated America's legal community during the glory days of the *Lochner* era. So how, then, did we end up with a social welfare state in America, where the feds have unchecked runaway power, the states comparatively little, and Americans have less freedoms?

Socialism was ascendant. For the sixty years following the New

Deal, its clouds have blocked the sun of freedom. How did this happen and why is it so incredibly dangerous? We will examine just this question in the coming chapters.

It is not a happy story.

8

THE LAST OF THE GOOD OLD DAYS

Just prior to President Franklin Delano Roosevelt's New Deal, there was a significant "moment" in constitutional history. It only lasted from 1935 to 1937, when the Supreme Court struck down several unconstitutional aspects of the president's legislative agenda. In this period, the Court searched for an "authentic" reading of the Constitution, particularly regarding the appropriate scope of federal authority to regulate both real and imagined commercial activity.

The Supreme Court has been portrayed as radical for striking down parts of the New Deal, but it was the circumstances, not the Court, that formed this impression. The truth is that during the years between the late 1800s and early 1900s, the Court's aggressive advancement of ideals like economic due process and a laissez faire economy were constructions of the law that were faithful to the Constitution. The Court vigorously enforced "freedom to choose." Sadly, the Court would soon retreat from upholding the Constitution and the Natural Law.

In 1937, the Court reversed course and began upholding New Deal legislation, and we've been feeling the effects of that retreat ever since. The modern Supreme Court's expansive reading of the Commerce Clause is but one example of the slippery slope created by the New Deal. Before the New Deal, the Commerce Clause was interpreted as giving Congress power to regulate interstate commerce, and to regulate intrastate matters provided that they substantially affected interstate commerce. "Production" and the "conditions of production" were reserved to the states because "commerce" only meant "the movement of goods." And under the Tenth Amendment, the states did not delegate to the federal government the power to regulate any other aspects of commercial activity.

Under principles espoused in the New Deal cases, the Court officially changed its position, eventually holding that the Commerce Clause allows regulation of production as well as movement of commercial goods,[1] no matter how minute or local.

PROVOKING THE BACKLASH

As we have seen in *Home Building & Loan Association v. Blaisdell* (1934), the Court upheld as constitutional a Minnesota moratorium on mortgages. This case was decided five to four, with the "Four horsemen" (the champions of opposition to the New Deal legislation), Justices Butler, McReynolds, Sutherland, and Van Devanter, dissenting.

In *Nebbia v. New York* (1934), the Court upheld as constitutional the price floor and price ceiling set by the State of New York for milk. Again, the Four Horsemen dissented.

It should be noted at the outset that Justice Roberts was critical to the outcome of this case (and he wrote for the majority). The four conservatives on the Court voted consistently to strike down federal regulations of economic matters other than true interstate commerce. The positions of Chief Justice Hughes and Justice Roberts, the two swing voters on the Court, determined the outcome of most of the early New Deal cases.

In 1934, the Horsemen dissented in both *Blaisdell* and *Nebbia*, which dealt with state regulatory legislation. But in *Railroad Retirement Board v. Alton Railroad* (1935), Justice Roberts swung to the conservative side of the Court, creating the majority to overrule the Railroad Pension Act.

The Court considered the question of whether "under the power to regulate commerce between the States Congress may require the carriers to make some provision for retiring and pensioning their employees." If so, then the Court would consider whether the provisions of the act bore a rational relation to regulating commerce. If not, Congress exceeded its constitutional bounds, and the Court must consider whether the remainder of the act could stand.

The federal government's goal in enacting the legislation was to promote "efficiency, economy, and safety." Thus, FDR argued that the act was a necessary and proper regulation of commerce, since the provisions were related to the main objective. He offered suggestions as to how the means justified the ends, but most of the justifications seemed to ignore the Constitution. For example, the government argued that providing a good retirement and pension plan would encourage old incompetent employees to retire, thus making the rails safer. That was actually the most compelling justification, and the Court dismissed it as being without constitutional substance.

In analyzing the case, the Court first examined the provisions of the act. Many were found to be arbitrary, capricious, and not rationally related to the goal of regulating commerce. The act contained a provision mandating pension eligibility for employees in the carrier's employ within one year prior to passage of the act, irrespective of future reemployment. The Court found that this provision was arbitrary. If upheld, it meant that railroad employers who had lawfully dismissed their employees within the previous year were required to provide pensions for them, *for life*.

The Court did not give much credence to the effects of employee happiness on interstate commerce. Justice Roberts wrote that if "'morale' is intended to connote efficiency, loyalty, and continuity of service, the surest way to destroy it in any privately owned business is to substitute legislative largess for private bounty and thus transfer the drive for pensions to the halls of Congress and transmute loyalty to employer into gratitude to the Legislature." When is the last time you heard that?!

Furthermore, while assuring an old age pension may boost morale, and high morale may promote efficiency, fostering a contented mind of an employee is "not a just regulation of interstate commerce." The Court wrote, "were this seen as a just regulation of interstate commerce Congress could mandate any action that would foster contented minds," e.g., pay raises, promotions, long vacations, nursery school, clothing, food; this is a list literally without end.

Finally, the Court concluded that the act was neither "in purpose [n]or effect a regulation of interstate commerce within the meaning of the Constitution." The ends simply did not square with the means. The Court observed that the main purpose of the act was not to secure the economic efficiency of the movement of goods across state borders, but rather to grant security and contentment to employees, and that is not area of behavior given to Congress to regulate. Though the act was arguably intended to encourage retirements, thus increasing employment by "providing a livable retirement for eligible railroad workers,"[2] it was one of a number of pieces of legislation in FDR's program that unduly involved the federal government in the management of businesses.

Justice Roberts called the act "an attempt for social ends to impose by sheer fiat non-contractual incidents upon the relation of employer and employee, not as a rule or regulation of commerce and transportation between the states, but as a means of assuring a particular class of employees against old age dependency."

That, he concluded, was "neither a necessary nor an appropriate rule or regulation affecting the due fulfillment of the railroads' duty to serve the public in interstate transportation." Justice Roberts wrote that the statute was "not in purpose or effect a regulation of interstate commerce within the meaning of the Constitution."

In 1933, Congress enacted the National Industrial Recovery Act, granting President Roosevelt the authority to promulgate "codes of fair competition" for particular industries as the need arose. The president himself did not create the codes; the industries were permitted to create the codes, thereby regulating themselves. The codes were approved or prescribed at the president's discretion, by executive order.

CHICKEN OR EGG ON THEIR FACES

In 1934, pursuant to the authority Congress gave him, FDR signed into law the Live Poultry Code. It fixed the maximum poultry industry workweek at forty hours per week; established a minimum wage of fifty cents per hour; established a minimum number of workers per plant based on the plant's weekly output; prohibited workers under the age of sixteen; and granted all workers the liberty to engage in collective bargaining.

The code was sponsored by the trade itself, which claimed it had been suffering from "uncontrolled methods of doing business." It was to be administered by an industry advisory committee, which would appoint a code supervisor. Administrative costs were to be borne by the industry, proportionate to revenue.

In 1935, New York had the biggest live poultry market in the country. Joseph, Martin, Alex, and Aaron Schechter together owned and operated two corporations. They purchased live poultry in New York City for slaughter and resale to distributors within New York who would sell directly to customers. They sold their poultry only from their slaughterhouses in Brooklyn. *They did not sell any poultry through interstate commerce.*

The federal government—which had never before regulated poultry—obtained an eighteen-count indictment against the Schechters. They were convicted of, among other things, violating the wage and hours provisions. They also failed to report their sales volume to the committee, sold an unfit chicken, sold chickens to unlicensed slaughterers and dealers, and sold chickens that had not been inspected.

The Schechters appealed their conviction, contending that the code was an unconstitutional use of legislative power to regulate in-state transactions and that this is the power of the state governments, not the federal government.

The Court of Appeals upheld sixteen of the eighteen convictions. The two counts pertaining to the wage and hours requirements were reversed, with the Court holding that Congress exceeded its regulatory authority in enacting these two provisions. Both the Schechters and the federal government appealed to the Supreme Court.

The federal government drew the Court's attention to the gravity of the nation's economic crisis, arguing that it warranted the statute authorizing the adoption of codes. FDR argued that the extraordinary nature of the times called for extraordinary remedies.

Chief Justice Hughes, writing for the majority, found that "extraordinary conditions do not create or enlarge constitutional power . . . the power of the national government is limited by constitutional grants." He conceded that the economic crisis qualified as an emergency, but reiterated that "emergency conditions, such as an economic crisis, may call for extraordinary remedies but they cannot create or enlarge constitutional powers."

The Court addressed the issue of interstate commerce. The Schechters purchased their chickens in Manhattan. They then drove their poultry to Brooklyn, where they prepared it for sale to local butchers who resold the chickens in Brooklyn. The Court declared, "Neither the slaughtering nor the sale were in interstate commerce."

The chickens may have been hatched out of state, and they may have been consumed out of state, but when they arrived in New York, the commerce came to a "permanent rest." Thus, the defendants' business had no interstate component, could not be characterized as interstate commerce, and so could not be regulated by the federal government.

The next inquiry was whether the business affected interstate commerce to the extent that it should be brought within the power of Congress under the Commerce Clause. The Court recognized that an intrastate activity could have enough of an effect on interstate commerce to warrant regulation, because whether or not something is in interstate commerce is not determined by the "source of the injury," but by the "effect on interstate commerce."

The Court drew a distinction between direct and indirect effects on interstate commerce, noting, "Where the effect of intrastate transactions on interstate commerce is indirect, the transactions remain the domain of state power." (This principle would later be repudiated in *Darcy* and *Wickard,* as we will explore later.)

The Court held that the law was invalid due to the attempt by Congress to regulate purely local matters.

A LUMP OF COAL FOR BIG GOVERNMENT REGULATORS

In *Carter v. Carter Coal Co.* (1936), finding that the Bituminous Coal Conservation Act of 1935 was primarily enacted to stabilize the mining industry through regulation of labor and prices, the Supreme Court ruled that mining was a local industry, the regulation of which was beyond the scope of the Commerce Clause. Furthermore, the Court found that the terms of the act affected production, not commerce.

The Bituminous Coal Act affected all coal miners in the country. The stated purposes of the act were to stabilize the coal industry and provide for interstate commerce, the general welfare, and conservation of resources.

The act created an excise tax on the sale of coal and a commission with the power to create the Coal Code, a series of regulations that would govern the industry. The code gave the commission the authority to set both minimum and maximum prices at every coal mine in the country and outlined the procedures for setting the prices.

Another contentious provision set wages. Stockholders of Carter Coal Co. brought a lawsuit to challenge the ability of the government to regulate the industry under the auspices of interstate commerce.

The Court held that the act did not regulate interstate commerce; rather, it was an attempt to regulate the coal mining industry because the provisions of the act applied regardless of whether the coal enters interstate commerce or not. "The stated general goals of the act, i.e., to provide for the general welfare and conserve the resource by controlling the production and distribution of coal, are of great worth, but Congress lacks constitutional power to implement them," Justice Sutherland wrote. "The federal government may only properly exercise enumerated powers."

The Court noted that it had consistently rejected the argument that the federal government can govern issues affecting the nation as a whole under the pretense that states cannot manage these issues by themselves and that Congress cannot claim powers that were not granted to it, expressly or implicitly.

The key inquiry was whether the Coal Conservation Act constituted regulation of interstate commerce. Commerce is intercourse—literally the movement of goods (a) out of one facility, (b) across state lines, and (c) into another facility—for the purposes of trade. The Congress's commerce power could never apply to purely internal transactions. Commerce is not manufacturing. Controlling manufacturing affects interstate commerce only secondarily; it is an indirect relationship. Thus, the Court held that mining is a local activity that does not constitute interstate commerce and can be regulated under local laws.

In *Carter Coal*, the Court properly defined "commerce." But it was one of sane constitutional interpretation's last gasps. If the Founders wanted Congress to be able to regulate intrastate activities with a minimal, indirect effect on commerce, then they would have included it in the enumerated powers of Congress. No such power exists, though. For one great moment, the Court recognized these facts and rightly upheld the Constitution.

All of this would soon change dramatically.

9

HOW BIG GOVERNMENT WON

After a series of five to four decisions in their favor, those who had trusted in the Constitution as a guarantor of limited government, natural rights, and free enterprise were beginning to become very nervous. They were right to worry, because one of the most powerful, strong-willed leaders of the century was about to pull a dirty trick out of his political hat, which would change everything. No matter how one feels about FDR, his political prowess and constitutional chicanery were undeniable.

The New Deal was a collection of regulations and agencies designed to pull us from the depths of the Great Depression, the Constitution not withstanding. Yet FDR's social welfare policies in many ways resemble the current assault on civil liberties by the Bush administration and the Congress. But did FDR understand the Constitution? Did FDR realize the long-term implications for human freedom of his New Deal? Did he care?

The New Deal may have helped some people in the short term, but it codified socialism, evaded the Constitution, disregarded the Natural Law, and put individualism on the path to extinction. No doubt, FDR boldly lead us out of the Great Depression and through the Second World War. Unfortunately, he did this in a most unconstitutional manner. And his successors followed his lead.

Due to the country's deep public reverence for the man, by 1937 the Supreme Court feared using the judicial review it had established in *Marbury*. Who then would tell Roosevelt that no matter how good his intentions were, they were, emphatically, not being carried out in a constitutional manner?

THE NEW DEAL COURT

At the beginning of Roosevelt's reign, much of his "progressive" legislation was found to be unconstitutional by the Court. The Four Horsemen, plus the swing vote of Justice Owen Roberts, upheld the Constitution when it conflicted with Roosevelt's legislation, just as the Marshall court did in *Marbury*.

But the Great Depression created pressure to abandon the Constitution's free market underpinnings. In this uniquely desperate time, popular perception was that government regulations would improve the economic state of those suffering, and when people are hungry, they tend not to think about the Constitution, limited government, or the Natural Law.

Legal Positivists gained intellectual prominence and attacked Natural Law principles that uphold freedom of contract and property rights. They argued instead that there were no natural rights to contract or to property and that the Court was simply making political choices that could be altered if the situation necessitated it.

Recall the landmark 1934 case, *Home Building & Loan Association v. Blaisdell.* There, the Court upheld a Minnesota law, a piece of New Deal legislation, which prevented mortgage holders from foreclosing on mortgages for a two-year period. As we discussed in an earlier chapter, this law was precisely the sort of legislation that the Contracts Clause was written to prevent, as it was passed to protect borrowers when they default by relieving them of their contractual obligations—their freely given agreement—to their lenders. The Court, nevertheless, upheld that law as "emergency legislation."

In *Blaisdell*, the Court flatly subordinated the Contracts Clause to whatever the Court and the legislature would deem a "valid police purpose." It also dismissed the Founders' intent for the Contracts Clause as being irrelevant in 1934. The code words "emergency legislation" and "valid police purpose" seem to be just what George Orwell warned us to watch out for in *1984*. Any time the government claims to be helping by way of an "emergency," it usually just means it is grabbing more power for itself, which means it is taking power from individuals. Ronald Reagan liked to say that the nine most dangerous words in the English language are: *"I'm from the government. I'm here to help you."*

In other words, the Court explicitly held that the Founders' intent is irrelevant in the interpretation of constitutional language! Therefore, the Constitution shall mean whatever the Court says it shall mean. Is not the whole purpose of a Constitution to insulate the limits it imposes on the government and the liberties it guarantees to individuals from the political winds that can animate an impatient majority? The Constitution is not some guideline to be consulted from time to time by politicians, lawmakers, and judges. *It is the supreme law of the land.*

Or it used to be, at any rate. Between 1937 and 1995, not a single federal law was declared unconstitutional by the Supreme Court. Not one piece of legislation was seen as exceeding the scope of Congress's commerce power. How did this happen? The Court adopted a deference to the legislature so extreme that the government's purpose does not need to be proved as the actual objective of the legislature; it need only be *hypothetically legitimate,* and not prohibited by the Constitution.

Hypothetically legitimate? Any parent could find some hypothetical reason to justify just about any rule to a child. But we are not children. And the government is certainly not our parents.

Socialists, like Norman Thomas, would have loved to see the government be our parents. He once boasted in the 1940s, "I have no need to run for president anymore, the Democratic Party has adopted my platform!" One of the two mainstream parties in the 1940s was pushing through socialist, anti-individualist, collectivist, unconstitutional legislation, and the Supreme Court allowed it!

The Court does have the power to keep things constitutional. Why doesn't it use that power? The answer lies in the momentum created by FDR's unchallenged New Deal.

After the *Blaisdell* case, the Court effectively gave up trying to uphold the Natural Law right to contract. Its new priority was "the common good" and making sure that the government would provide for it. The Court also distanced itself from its role as a check on Congress and a guard of legislative constitutionality. "Whether the free operation of the normal laws of competition is a wise and wholesome rule for trade and commerce is an economic question that this court need not consider or determine . . . [and one with which] the courts are both incompetent and unauthorized to deal." That lovely sentiment is from the *Blaisdell* dissent.

The Supreme Court began to bow to political pressures in 1934 when New York adopted a Milk Control law that established a board empowered to set a minimum retail price for milk. Nebbia was a storeowner who sold milk *below* the minimum price. He sold it cheaper than the State wished. In *Nebbia v. New York* (1934), the Court reversed the premise that government could only regulate to achieve a narrow and valid police purpose so long as it does not interfere with the constitutionally granted rights of freedom of contract and freedom of property.

"The state is free to adopt whatever economic policy may reasonably be deemed to promote public welfare and to enforce that policy by legislation adapted to its purpose." The Court held there was nothing "peculiarly sacrosanct" about milk prices that insulated them from government regulation and upheld the law. What happened to the Contracts Clause? What happened to free enterprise? Is it not good for consumers—the common good—to pay less for milk rather than more?

The Supreme Court also made a complete departure from *Lochner*'s rationale. The Court wrote that the evils in the market "could not be expected to right themselves through the ordinary play of the forces of supply and demand." In constitutional terms, the Court wrongly stated that "Neither property rights nor contract rights are absolute. . . . Equally fundamental with the private right is that of the public to regulate it in the common interest." From this point on, the *Lochner* concept of the Constitution as guarantor of freedom of individual action from government interference was a dead letter.

FDR'S DIRTY POLITICAL TRICK

To ensure that the Court would continue in the vein of *Nebbia* and fall in line with the political demands of the times, Roosevelt and his attorney general concocted a plan that would dramatically alter the course of his presidency, and the nation's history.[1]

The president proposed increasing the number of justices on the Supreme Court and in the federal judiciary. Roosevelt's initial plan would have allowed him to appoint a new justice if a sitting one continued to serve beyond six months after his seventieth birthday. This would have allowed him to add up to six justices to the Supreme Court for a total of fifteen, as well as forty-four judges to the federal trial and appellate courts.

The plan became the most contentious national issue since the Civil War, and it was by far the most significant challenge to judicial authority since the Marshall era. It drew intense opposition, even from supporters of the New Deal programs, because it was a threat to the independence of the judiciary and to the Constitution itself.

In the midst of congressional, editorial, and public reaction to the "court packing" plan, and perhaps as a result of it, the year 1937 saw cases involving both substantive due process and the scope of the Congress's commerce power that brought about a new era of the federal government's paternalism and a massive expansion of federal government power that saddles and socializes Americans to this day.

NO PROCESS DUE

Justice Owen Roberts switched ideological sides and brought a conclusive end to the Constitution as protector of natural rights, the free market, and federalism, which had characterized the Court's decisions for the preceding 150 years. His decisive vote as part of the five to four majority against many minimum wage programs swung the other way to become the five to four majority in *West Coast Hotel v. Parrish,* in favor of minimum wage programs. Robert's change will forever be known as "the switch in time that saved nine." The court-packing plan was withdrawn.

Clearly, Roosevelt had won the battle to keep the courts from invalidating his legislation by threatening to dilute the ranks of judges and justices who disagreed with his understanding of the Constitution. Imagine the audacity of a president trying to alter the entire federal judiciary in order to intimidate a justice into switching ideological sides? Talk about dirty politics. Talk about utter disregard for the Constitution. Talk about "torturing" a sacred document. Talk about it all you want. It worked.

Then the assault on the Constitution began in earnest. The State of New York had passed a minimum wage law for female employees. But Elsie Parrish, an employee of the West Coast Hotel Company, still received subminimum wage compensation for her work. Parrish sued to recover the difference between the wages paid to her and the minimum wage fixed by state law.

In *West Coast Hotel v. Parish* (1937), the members of the newly realigned majority on the Supreme Court upheld the federal establishment of minimum wages for women. They made perfectly clear that the principles of substantive due process in *Lochner v. New York* were abandoned. The Constitution would no longer be used to protect economic liberties.

Chief Justice Hughes, writing for the majority, stated, "The Constitution does not speak of freedom of contract. It speaks of liberty and prohibits the deprivation of liberty without due process of law. The liberty safeguarded (in the Due Process Clause) is liberty in a social organization which requires the protection of law against the evils which menace the health, safety, morals, and welfare of the people. . . ." Whatever happened to the Contracts Clause?

Nor would the freedom of contract be safeguarded as a fundamental right and given the highest degree of constitutional protection by the Supreme Court. In "Constitution speak" that means that the government is free to regulate in the economic realm as long as its purpose is legitimate. The Court opined, "Freedom of contract is a qualified, and not an absolute, right. There is no absolute freedom to do as one wills or to contract as one chooses. The guaranty of liberty does not withdraw from legislative supervision . . . the making of contracts, or deny to government the power to provide restrictive safeguards." Where did this come from? I'll give you a hint: not from the Constitution or its Contracts Clause.

Congress was now set to become the paternalistic, legislative watchdog, guarding individuals from the "evils" of free market activity. The federal judiciary would now defer to Congress as long as the laws and regulations were "reasonable." But what would constitute "reasonable"? We were headed down the slippery slope to the modern social welfare state.

To offend further, in *United States v. Carolene Products Co.* (1938), the Court upheld the federal government's Filled Milk Act of 1923, which banned the interstate shipment of "filled milk" (milk with skimmed milk and vegetable oil added). Now the power to regulate (to make regular) interstate commerce includes the power to ban products not intrinsically harmful, but just distasteful; distasteful in Congress's opinion.

The Court went even further in this case than it did in *Parish* and said that economic regulations need only have "any conceivable" rational basis, regardless of Congress's actual intent. That is, *as long as the Court or the government's lawyers defending the statute can drum up any hypothetical congressional intention for passing a law that would serve a rational end, it would pass constitutional muster.* Federal law was now in the imaginations of whatever a member of Congress or federal judge or government lawyer could "conceive" it to be. The torturing of the Constitution continued. No wonder it would soon be banished into exile.

A FOOTNOTE RESCUES THE CONSTITUTION

Carolene Products essentially created the presumption that any economic regulation was constitutional. A famous footnote in this case creates the only guideline for when judicial deference to Congress would become a "more searching judicial scrutiny."

When a law discriminates against "discrete and insular minorities" (like the board of education did against African Americans in *Brown*) or interferes with "individual rights" (like the Connecticut legislature did to property ownership in *Calder*) or restricts the political process from repealing undesirable legislation; in other words, when it violates only a certain class of natural rights, what the Court, not nature, calls "fundamental," these would be the only circumstances that would invite a heightened inquiry and scrutiny from the Court.

In sum, the Supreme Court made it clear that free enterprise, which encompasses the natural right to enter into an enforceable agreement, and the right to use and exclude persons from private property, notwithstanding the fact that it is explicitly spoken of by the Founders in the Constitution and in the Declaration of Independence, are not among those individual rights that would receive meaningful protection from the judiciary. Where did these rights go? Into exile.

A SOP TO CONGRESS

In *NLRB v. Jones & Laughlin Steel Corp.* (1937), the Court overruled the limits it had placed on Congress's commerce power. The National Labor Relations Act of 1935 established the National Labor Relations Board to oversee labor disputes. Congress determined that labor-management disputes were directly related to the flow of interstate commerce and, thus, could be regulated by the federal government. The production-versus-commerce distinction was thus discarded.

In this case, the NLRB charged Jones & Laughlin with violating the act by engaging in unfair labor practices by discriminating against members of the union with regard to hire and tenure of employees, and coercing and intimidating its employees so as to interfere with their organization.

The National Labor Relations Board ordered Jones & Laughlin to cease and desist from such discrimination and coercion and offer reinstatement to all employees that the company had discharged. There were 10 of them; 10 out of 560,000 employees. Could the treatment of the 10 possibly have affected interstate commerce?

The steel industry challenged the power of Congress to establish the Board, and the actions taken by it, as well as the constitutionality of the act itself. The Court upheld the Board's actions and the constitutionality of the act and ruled that the National Labor Relations Board may regulate those industrial activities, which had the "*potential* to burden or restrict interstate commerce."

To quote Ronald Reagan, "There you go again!" The Court stood by while Congress created code words and phrases like "potential to burden" commerce. Doesn't just about everything fall into that category?

In this decision, the Court's new majority turned its due process doctrine ruling, as articulated in *Lochner* and *Carter,* on its head. And it completely discarded its position that labor relations had only an indirect effect on commerce. (Certainly firing 10 out of 560,000 employees has no direct effect on interstate commerce.) To make matters worse, the same Court that had yet to define the right *to work* as "fundamental," and thus entitled to protection from the judiciary, said the right *to organize a labor union* was "fundamental."

The Court also said the federal government had the right to intervene in labor disputes. The Supreme Court would now allow Congress to pass legislation that would attempt to equalize bargaining power between employers and their employees. "The exploitation of a class of workers who are in an unequal position with respect to bargaining power and are thus relatively defenseless . . . casts a burden for their support upon the community." Doesn't that sound more like Karl Marx than Thomas Jefferson? The justices went so far as to state that the national government was justified in penalizing corporations engaging in interstate commerce which "refuse to confer and negotiate" with their workers as a group. And that is where in the Constitution?

These judicial about-faces were no doubt a reaction to the disastrous economic circumstances of the time and the court-packing stunt much more so than they were true reflections of what is actually a fundamental right under the Constitution.

One of the most important pieces of constitutional vocabulary to be assigned a new meaning at this time was the term "commerce." The Court flatly declared that "the fact the employees . . . were engaged in production is not determinative." The power of Congress would be exerted to protect interstate commerce "no matter what the source of the dangers that threatens it" regardless of whether that source was production, manufacturing, or trade. The "production" versus "commerce" distinction was discarded.

The Court began to exceed even Chief Justice Marshall's views on the Commerce Clause. The federal government, though limited in its powers, is supreme within its field, and the power of Congress over interstate commerce is plenary, notwithstanding the states' inherent interest in regulating for health, safety, welfare, and morality (the "police power") that is recognized by the Ninth and Tenth Amendments. The Court declared that "The fundamental principle is that the power to regulate commerce is the power to enact all appropriate legislation for its protection and advancement."

Justice McReynolds, one of the Four Horsemen, at this point a lone horseman, vehemently dissented in *Jones & Laughlin.* He argued that the reinstatement of these employees only affected about ten people directly, so any relation or effect on commerce was remote and indirect. He even lamented that if the distinction between direct and indirect is obliterated, then almost anything—birth, death, marriage—might affect commerce and thus be subject to congressional regulation.

Recently, U.S. Court of Appeals Judge Douglas Ginsburg wrote that "judges were faithful to the Constitution for most of the nation's history—from the founding, in fact, through the first third of the twentieth century. But sometime in the 1930s, the wheels began to come off."

Judge Ginsburg's criticism of the Supreme Court's jurisprudential history is aimed at its 1937 decision to uphold the National Labor Relations Act. Judge Ginsburg objects that it was "loose reasoning" and an extreme and "stark break from the Court's precedent." And, as far as I know, it was Judge Ginsburg who first coined the phrase I have used as the main title of this book: The Constitution in Exile.

A CONSTITUTIONAL STEAMROLLING

In the same year, the Court, now riding on a constitutional steamroller it seemed unable to stop, upheld a law that placed a double tax burden on business owners simply to promote the "general welfare" as part of the Social Security Act. The act established a federal payroll tax on employers. However, if employers paid taxes to a state unemployment compensation fund (which was created by the states and was subject to federal standards), they were allowed to credit those payments toward the federal tax.

In *Steward Machine Company v. Davis* (1937), the Steward

Machine Company challenged the validity of this tax. The Court stated that the tax under the Social Security Act was a constitutional exercise of congressional power, and not a subversion of the principles of federalism and the rights reserved to the states as it had stated in *United States v. Butler* just one year earlier, and in *Drexel Furniture*, just a few years earlier. Employers would now be responsible to the states for the tax, as well as to the federal government. That is twice the burden for employers in a state that requires the employers to pay this unemployment tax.

The Court simply held that "the nation was responding to the call of the distressed" and was benefiting from the "larger freedom from economic chaos." Where did they get this stuff? The stated place was the Commerce Clause. Can you see it there? I don't.

In 1938, Congress continued to expand its own power and passed the Fair Labor Standards Act to regulate many aspects of employment including minimum wages, maximum weekly hours, and child labor. It should have been called the Unfair Taking of Your Freedoms Act of 1938 because, under the guise of setting fair labor standards (how many union members voted for the Democrats?), Congress destroyed the freedom of workers and employers *to agree*, and the Supreme Court found nothing in the Constitution to impede this.

The law prohibited the interstate shipment of goods made by manufacturers who violated the maximum hour and minimum wage requirements set up by the act. Corporations that set their own employment standards and produced goods to be sold in other states were punished for shipping the goods to other states.

In *United States v. Darby* (1941), a now unanimous Supreme Court affirmed the right of Congress to exercise "to its utmost extent" the powers reserved for it in the Commerce Clause, and again upheld the Fair Labor Standards Act. The Court held that

Congress acted with proper authority in outlawing substandard labor conditions since they have a significant impact on interstate commerce. In a Marxist spirit, the Court rejected substantive due process arguments as well as arguments advocating the limited power of Congress. It also expressly rejected the view that the Constitution left production for the states to regulate, or that the Natural Law left it to individual choices to regulate.

"The shipment of manufactured goods interstate is such commerce, and the production of such shipments by Congress is indubitably a regulation of commerce." By this the Supreme Court had overruled the production/commerce distinction and the directness and indirectness test of *Carter Coal* and *Hammer v. Dagenhart.* The steamrolling, shredding, and torturing of the Constitution by the Congress and the Courts was in full swing. But could the document survive the assault?

In disregarding the Natural Law, the Court dramatically rejected the view that the Tenth Amendment limits Congress's power. The holding in *Darby* emasculated and nullified the meaning of the Tenth Amendment. The most infamous quote goes like this: "The Amendment states but a truism that all is retained that has not been surrendered." The Tenth Amendment would no longer be used by the federal courts to invalidate federal laws in order to protect the zone of power left to the states.

Any congressional regulation would now be regarded as constitutional if that regulation were reasonable (in the minds of the members of Congress who wrote it or the government lawyers who defended it or the federal judges who interpreted it) in order to bring about federal control of any aspect of interstate commerce. Congress would thus have plenary power to establish the terms and circumstances for the interstate shipment of goods (and just about anything else it wants to regulate, control, or stifle).

Justice Stone wrote for the Court that the "motive and purpose of a regulation of interstate commerce are matters for the legislative judgment . . . over which the courts are given *no* control" (emphasis added). The only restriction for such legislative judgment would be the impairment of a fundamental right or liberty, and economic liberties were simply not fundamental.

The Court states that if no fundamental liberty is impaired, there only need be a rational basis—any rational basis—for the promotion of a legitimate congressional or commercial end. The fact that other noncongressional or noncommercial ends, even ends not within the enumerated powers of Congress, might also be achieved, does not affect the constitutionality of a congressional scheme.

Darby drove home the Court's radical about-face. The federal government would be accorded incredibly broad powers to regulate the national economy, so much so that states may even be barred from regulating *intrastate* commerce.

THE FOUR HORSEMEN RIDE INTO THE SUNSET

Between 1937 and 1941, the Four Horsemen and others left the Supreme Court. Roosevelt ultimately made eight appointments to the Supreme Court, the most of any president except Washington. The Court was now in line with the New Deal's programs and legislation. And it would stay there until 1995.

Justice McReynolds, one of the Four Horsemen, dissented 119 times from 1937 until his resignation in 1941. Justice McReynolds became the lone symbol of constitutional and Natural Law freedom on the Supreme Court, and while he may have been singular on the Court, he was not alone in society or history.

After the court-packing plan, FDR never had the level of public support he enjoyed in the 1936 election. He never had the power on the Hill that he once had. His foreign policy may have been adversely affected as well. He also hurt the credibility of the Court. Lingering questions about the Court's independence and neutrality remain to this day.

GOVERNMENT INTRUSIONS INTO OTHER AREAS BEGIN

The Positivist Court's newly embraced deference to the legislature made it possible for the Court to take a number of jurisprudential paths that would have been unheard of during the hands-off approach from 1789 to 1937.

A famous example occurred in 1939, when the Court used Congress's newly expanded power under the Commerce Clause to undermine the Second Amendment. In *United States v. Miller* (1939), the Court gave authority to the claim that the Second Amendment merely guarantees a collective right of states to maintain militias, and does not guarantee to individuals the right to bear arms.

The case involved the indictment of Jack Miller and a cohort for unlawfully transporting in interstate commerce a double barrel 12-gauge shotgun, contrary to the National Firearms Act of 1934. When the case was at the trial court, Miller's attorney filed a motion to dismiss the indictment on the grounds that the portion of the National Firearms Act under which Miller had been charged usurped the power reserved to the states and violated the Second Amendment. The trial judge granted the motion, and the charges against Miller were dismissed.

The power hungry feds, however, filed an appeal directly to the Supreme Court. When the case was argued, only the government was represented, which of course advocated for the validity of the act.

The Supreme Court in *Miller* sent the case back to the trial court to decide whether a short-barreled shotgun is the type of firearm protected by Second Amendment. The Court discussed the origins of the Second Amendment as follows: "The Constitution as originally adopted granted to the Congress power to provide for calling forth the Militia to execute the Laws of the Union, suppress Insurrections and repel Invasions; To provide for organizing, arming, and disciplining, the Militia . . . in the Service of the United States, reserving to the States respectively, the Appointment of the Officers, and the Authority of training the Militia according to the discipline prescribed by Congress."

This case has been routinely read by gun-prohibitionists and antigun judges to mean that the Second Amendment merely provides for a well regulated militia, not the right of an individual to keep and bear arms in his own defense, specifically a weapon such as a double barrel 12-gauge shotgun.

Many years after FDR's death, Columbia Law School Professor Rexford G. Tugwell, who had been at the core of FDR's braintrust in the New Deal era, made a startling admission. Referring to the New Deal's utter disregard for the Constitution, he said: "To the extent that these [New Deal] policies developed, they were *the tortured interpretations* of a document [i.e., the Constitution] intended to prevent them."[3] Wow.

FDR's New Dealism had begun to spill over into every area of human endeavor. So just how much freedom have we lost from the New Deal? We will start to answer that question in the next chapter by addressing how much can be regulated in the name of commerce, and just what happened in 1995 to return freedom to constitutional jurisprudence.

10

COMMERCE, COMMERCE EVERYWHERE

The feds have grown strong thanks to congressmen and senators from both major American political parties giving power to the government that is not enumerated, delegated, specified, contemplated, or even hinted at in the Constitution. Thanks to the dereliction of duty of the Supreme Court in sanctioning these unjust laws, just about every area of human endeavor and behavior is now regulated by the federal government "in the name of commerce."

Against the tide of recent history, the Rehnquist court attempted to revitalize the concept of federalism. The Court's ability to do so, however, was limited by the pro-Big Government bias of some justices and their willingness to continue to accept as valid much of the precedent from the New Deal era.

The Supreme Court changed course during the New Deal, ignoring nearly a century of cases which in the Commerce Clause *limited* the ability of the federal government to hinder the freedom of individuals. At first, when the Congress began passing New Deal legislation that increased the powers of the federal government, the Court struck down the laws because they exceeded the scope of Congress's power under the Commerce Clause. Then, in 1937, it simply abrogated its role and stopped enforcing the Constitution's limits on federal power.

Professor Richard Epstein considers the New Deal a "sharp departure" from earlier case law. Beginning in the 1990s, however the Rehnquist Court started to move the pendulum of jurisprudence in the other direction. Whether the pendulum continues to move under new Chief Justice John G. Roberts Jr. remains to be seen.

GIBBONS IN DECLINE

So how did we get to a place where Congress seemingly can restrict and regulate nearly every form of human activity? Lawmakers frequently cite *Gibbons* as a case that gives Congress broad power to regulate commerce. Under that case, Congress even regulates objects that only indirectly affect commerce between the states. However, the Court's opinion in *Gibbons* has been misunderstood. The *Gibbons* Court only wanted to say that Congress has broad power to regulate the specific objects that fall under the Commerce Clause.[1] Chief Justice Marshall, writing for the majority of the Court, suggested that "It is therefore the nature of a transaction, rather than its location, that stamps it as part of interstate commerce." Marshall was only saying that Congress clearly has the power to regulate certain things, such as interstate commerce.

Marshall did write that "This power, like all others vested in Congress, is complete in itself, may be exercised to its utmost extent, and acknowledges no limitations other than are prescribed in the [C]onstitution." However, he qualified his remarks by saying, "the sovereignty of Congress, though limited to specified objects, [in the Constitution] is plenary as to those objects. . . ."

Marshall rejected the proposition that Congress could pass

inspection laws under the Commerce Clause. He explained, "inspection laws really dealt with objects before they became a part of interstate commerce, and thus were not properly situated within the realm of interstate commerce."

The present use of the Commerce Clause to impose broad regulations while relying on Marshall's precedent is not consistent with Marshall's own articulated understanding of the Commerce Clause. Marshall clearly said, "there are things too far attenuated from interstate commerce to be held as 'affecting' it, despite the fact that for example, objects are inspected because they will become a part of interstate commerce." So what are these "things," Mr. Chief Justice?

The case of *United States v. E.C. Knight* (1895), which has been cited as rigid, formalistic, and an impediment to congressional exercise of its power, is perfectly in line with Marshall's exposition of Commerce Clause principles in *Gibbons*. At issue in *E.C. Knight* was the Sherman Anti-Trust Act, which was passed by Congress. The act attempted to outlaw monopolies and noncompetitive business practices. After the federal government tried to prevent mergers between companies that controlled 98 percent of the American sugar industry, the companies brought a lawsuit. The Court held that the act was a valid exercise of Congress's power under the Commerce Clause, but that it did not apply to manufacturing.

However, since it is supposed to be the high watermark of the period in terms of the Court's refusal to include manufacturing in interstate commerce, it is in line with *Gibbons*. *E.C. Knight* said that manufacturing was not commerce, and the fact that an object was intended for interstate commerce did not make it an article of interstate commerce before or after its travel. The changes after the New Deal were not a "return" to Marshall's stated vision of the scope and operation of the clause; they were a sharp turn away from precedent.

It seems that the Court's first break from the traditional approach to the Commerce Clause occurred in *NLRB v. Jones & Laughlin Steel Corp.*, when the Court advanced the argument that anything which affected commerce, regardless of the source, could be regulated under the Commerce Clause. The Court muddled the distinction between manufacturing and commerce. In subsequent cases, the Court pointed to the difficulty in dealing with competition between states as a reason for regulation.[2]

AN ATTEMPT TO RIGHT A BIG WRONG

On March 10, 1992, a twelfth-grade student named Alfonso Lopez was arrested because he carried a "concealed .38 caliber handgun and five bullets" with him to Edison High school in San Antonio, Texas. What conceivable federal issue could be implicated by these events? Wait.

The federal government claimed that Lopez intended to sell the gun to another student. When school authorities were informed that he had a gun and approached him, Lopez confessed to having the weapon. After his arrest, Lopez was charged with possessing a firearm on school grounds, in violation of Texas law. On the day after his arrest, the state charges—the ones for which he admitted his guilt—were dropped, and Lopez was indicted under the *federal* Gun-Free School Zones Act.

The feds wanted in on the prosecution, as they do in everything these days.

In 1990, Congress had passed the Gun-Free School Zones Act. The bill was introduced in the House by Rep. Edward Feighan, Democrat of Ohio, and the Congressional Record suggests the bill was passed in response to increasing national levels of violent crime.

Certainly, we want children to be safe in school, but do we need the feds to do it? Does Congress have the power to do it? Do not state laws suffice?

Records indicate that Feighan introduced the bill in 1989 by talking about "terrified children, frightened parents, and horrified teachers." He mentioned four separate violent incidents in schools around the country. Representative Feighan then cited a number of statistics indicating how many children take guns to school per day and how many children skip school as a result of the fear of violence. Finally, he noted that schools were having to prepare children for the possibility of violent outbreaks.

After apprising his colleagues of these conditions he said, "That is why I am today introducing legislation to create gun-free school zones." This sentence immediately follows his accounts of violence and the terror and fear it induces inside our nation's schools.[3]

The bill made it a violation of federal law for someone to possess a gun in a school zone. Alfonso Lopez was convicted under the act and received a sentence of six months in prison, followed by two years of parole. Congrats to the feds for stealing more power from the states!

After Lopez was tried in front of a federal magistrate judge and found guilty, he appealed his conviction twice. His appeal was denied in district court. Lopez persisted, though, arguing that Congress had no power to regulate crime where there was no federal property or interstate commerce involved. The Fifth Circuit Court of Appeals reversed his conviction, a ruling that was sustained by the Supreme Court in a five to four decision.

Amazingly, the lawyers for the federal government did not attempt any of their usual complicated maneuvers to argue that the act was intended to regulate interstate commerce. The legislative history was too damning. They could not deny that the purpose of the regulation was to reduce violent crimes in schools. In fact, they conceded that none of the legislative history referenced the effects of guns in school zones on interstate commerce. Instead they simply said that the legislation was permissible because possession of a firearm in a school zone did "substantially affect" interstate commerce. What? How on earth did it supposedly do so?

The federal prosecutors—now humiliated that they had an obviously guilty defendant on their hands whose state prosecutors they had bullied into dismissing the case and whose federal conviction had been thrown out—claimed guns in schools substantially affected interstate commerce by increasing the costs of insurance throughout the population and by reducing travel to areas that are perceived of as unsafe. Guns in school zones hamper the educational process, reducing productivity and ultimately economic well-being, but bringing a gun into a school is hardly a commercial activity.

Writing for the majority, Chief Justice Rehnquist questioned the implications of the government's arguments, specifically the possibility of conflating a state's police power with federal Commerce Clause power. If the federal government's arguments were accepted, any federal regulation of violent crime would be permissible under the Commerce Clause.

The *Lopez* Court said that to grant Congress the power to regulate crime under the Commerce Clause would be to "convert congressional authority under the Commerce Clause to a general police power of the sort retained by the States" under the Constitution.

The Court characterized the history of Commerce Clause regulation in a very clear manner, identifying three main periods in the development of Commerce Clause jurisprudence. The first century of cases was viewed as defining how the Commerce Clause limited state legislation that "discriminated against interstate commerce."

The next half-century, from 1887 to 1936, was seen as limiting congressional power to regulate production, manufacturing, and mining. In other words, the cases honored the definition of commerce by excluding these activities from it. Thus the boundaries of congressional power were being defined. This period also permitted Congress to regulate purely intrastate activity where "interstate and intrastate commerce" were so commingled that the regulation of one necessitated the incidental regulation of the other.

While this seemed to expand congressional authority, the Court clearly distinguished between direct and indirect effects, providing limits to the scope of Congress's power.

The next period, starting in 1937 with *NLRB v. Jones & Laughlin*, eliminated the need to distinguish between indirect and direct effects. What a stretch! All that was required for regulation of purely intrastate activities was a showing of a "close and substantial" relation to interstate commerce. The *Lopez* Court said that *NLRB* "ushered in an era of Commerce Clause jurisprudence that greatly expanded the previously defined authority of Congress under that Clause." I could not agree more.

Finally, the Rehnquist Court concluded with the observation that there are three categories of permissible regulation under the Commerce Clause. First, Congress may regulate the use of the "channels of interstate commerce," like interstate highways and railroads. Second, it may "regulate and protect" the "instrumentalities of interstate commerce, or persons or things in interstate commerce," like the vehicles in which the goods or persons are physically located when they move across state borders, even if the danger comes from "purely intrastate activities." Third, Congress may regulate activities having a "substantial relation" to interstate commerce. Despite conflicting precedent, the Court concluded that the activity being regulated must "substantially affect" (rather than just "affect") interstate commerce.

The Court said that the behavior in question that the Congress sought to prohibit (carrying a gun into a school) "did not fall" into either the first or second category of activity. The Court considered if and how the behavior in question may fit within the third category of permissible regulation under the Commerce Clause.

To make its assessment, the Court articulated a "pattern" in cases which held that an activity "substantially affects interstate commerce." The pattern would become the test for which this case is often cited.

Economic activities were generally sustained because they substantially affect interstate commerce. But there is one inescapable truism that was fatal to the government's argument here: there was no economic or commercial enterprise at issue in the *Lopez* case.

Regulations containing a clause limiting their effect only to interstate commerce were sometimes upheld, as they actually affected interstate commerce. If the law had made a connection with interstate commerce by saying that it was a crime to attempt to sell a gun that was transported via interstate commerce in a school zone, it could be constitutional. But, if the relationship between the activity and interstate commerce is attenuated, the Court would not find a substantial effect.

The federal law in *Lopez* failed each of these tests, thus, the Court held that the Congress exceeded its authority in enacting the legislation. Finally, after sixty years of abuse, the torture of the Commerce Clause ended. The Court clearly stated, "The act exceeds Congress' Commerce Clause authority. First, although this Court has upheld a wide variety of congressional Acts regulating intrastate economic activity that substantially affected interstate commerce, the possession of a gun in a local school zone is in no sense an economic activity that might, through repetition elsewhere, have such a substantial effect on interstate commerce."

The dissent, authored by Justice Breyer, starts with the premise that the Congress can regulate virtually any activity it wants. In determining whether there is a substantial effect on interstate commerce, Breyer cited the principle that the cumulative effect of individual activities causes an effect on interstate commerce.

Justice Breyer used this reasoning to argue that the Court should consider the cumulative effect, not the individual instance. Amazingly, he stretched, "in determining whether a local activity will likely have a significant effect upon interstate commerce, a court must consider, not the effect of an individual act (a single instance of gun possession), but rather the cumulative effect of all similar instances (i.e., the effect of all guns possessed in or near schools)."

FOLLOWING SUIT IN RESCUING THE COMMERCE CLAUSE

Similarly, *Morrison v. United States* (2000) tested the constitutionality of an act of Congress that "created a private right of action for victims of gender violence" against their assailants. Congress had attempted to make rape a federal crime, based partially on the fact that rape victims are frequently absent from work while they recover, which affects interstate commerce. How far we have come from regulating ferries between Hoboken and Manhattan!

Congress had actually gone further in this case than in *Lopez* to establish the link between gender-violence and commerce. It commissioned studies which demonstrated that "the failure of states to control gender-related violence harmed the economic prospects of citizens, particularly women." Thus, Congress concluded, the violence affected interstate commerce.

The Court also rejected this argument. Relying on *Lopez*, Chief Justice Rehnquist wrote that "Congress could not regulate non-economic activity." And that excludes violence.

In 2000, the Supreme Court decided *Jones v. United States.* In 1998, Dewey Jones set fire to his cousin's private home in Indiana. The fire caused serious damage to the house, although no one was injured. Jones was prosecuted under a federal law prohibiting arson with respect to any "property used in interstate or foreign commerce or in any activity affecting interstate or foreign commerce."

Jones was convicted under the federal law and sentenced to thirty-five years in prison pursuant to federal guidelines. He unsuccessfully appealed to the U.S. Court of Appeals for the Seventh Circuit, arguing that the application of the federal law to the arson of a private home exceeded the scope of congressional authority under the Commerce Clause. The Supreme Court reversed the decision, saying that the statute "does not reach an owner-occupied residence that is not used for any commercial purpose."

One might wonder how it ever got this far. How could any court construe the words "used in . . . or . . . affecting . . . commerce" to include a private home? The government apparently posited that the house was used in three ways that affected commerce. "The homeowner used the dwelling as collateral" to secure an Oklahoma mortgage. He also "used" it to obtain a casualty insurance policy from a Wisconsin insurer. And the homeowner "used" it to receive natural gas from sources outside of Indiana.

The Court did not find a problem with the government's attempt to satisfy the "affecting commerce" requirement. Rather the problem was with the word "used." The Court ruled that "used" in the statute necessitates "active employment with." The residence is not really "used" in the appropriate sense through any of the aforementioned purposes.

Writing for the majority, the normally liberal, loose-constructionist Justice Ginsburg aptly noted that "Were we to adopt the Government's expansive interpretation of 844(i), hardly a building in the land would fall outside the federal statute's domain. Practically every building in our cities, towns, and rural areas is constructed with supplies that have moved in interstate commerce, served by utilities that have an interstate connection, financed or insured by enterprises that do business across state lines, or has some other trace of interstate commerce."

Later in the opinion, Justice Ginsberg did say that the Court would decline to answer the constitutional question of whether "traditionally local criminal conduct" is a "matter for federal enforcement."

As we have seen in all of these cases, Congress is hungry for power and has found the Commerce Clause to be a convenient bottomless pit for increasing its regulatory powers. Congress will undoubtedly keep trying to impose laws on the American public while hiding behind the Commerce Clause. Hopefully, the Supreme Court will continue the recent trend initiated by *Lopez, Morrison,* and *Jones* will uphold the true intent of the Constitution.

11

FROM WHEAT TO WEED

This chapter is about wheat, power, pot, and perversion. This is the story of just how loony the Congress and Supreme Court have become in dictating the way you live your life. They have moved us to the most un-American way of life: federal government central planning of your backyard garden. You have to wonder what they are smoking.

Citing Pope John Paul II, Professor Rice wrote that what is best for a person cannot be determined without him having the ability to make decisions for himself. Rice also noted that the Pope believed that socialism conflicts with Judeo-Christian principles because it denies the individual the ability to make choices. The Pope held that *that* is the essence of individual freedom: the ability to make choices.

Regardless, socialism was on the rise in America for much of the twentieth century. In 1938, Congress enacted the Agricultural Adjustment Act to control the supply and thereby the price of wheat traveling across state and national borders. The government sought to "avoid surpluses and shortages," and more importantly, to avoid price fluctuations.

The act enabled the secretary of agriculture to determine via a quota system how much wheat each farmer could grow. At the same time, under Stalin's rule the central planners in Moscow were dictating to farmers all over the USSR how much wheat they could produce.

The American secretary of agriculture set the national wheat allotment, just as his Soviet counterpart did. The American allotment divided wheat among the states, then among counties and individual farmers, just as Soviet allotments did.

In May 1941, the secretary of agriculture publicly announced an increase in the costs of loans for planting wheat. He did not say that the penalty for producing wheat in excess of the quota was also increasing. The secretary did say that, considering the situation in the world, "farmers should not be penalized because they have provided insurance against food shortages."

OVERPRODUCE AND PAY

Roscoe Filburn was a farmer in Ohio. He owned a dairy farm that also grew a modest amount of wheat. The wheat was used to feed cattle, was consumed by him and his family, or was used for seed. It never left his farm.

In July 1940, the federal government told Filburn that he could grow 11.1 acres of wheat. He grew 23 acres of wheat, though, and this violated the quota.

Under the act, Filburn was fined $117.11 for producing wheat in excess of the quota. He could have paid the fine or just stored the excess wheat, but he instead decided to challenge the law, as the amount of the fine had been increased *after* he had planted the wheat.

The trial court held in favor of Filburn. The excess wheat that he grew was intended for use on his farm and thus did not appear to violate the act. Unfortunately, the secretary of agriculture appealed the case.

The Supreme Court held in favor of the secretary, reversing the lower court's decision. Justice Jackson wrote the majority opinion, which examined the regulation of purely intrastate activity by Congress under the Commerce Clause and whether production was an activity that could be validly regulated under the Commerce Clause.

Filburn's main argument was that his case did not fall under "the regulatory power of the Commerce Clause" because he was not engaged in interstate commerce. Filburn pointed out that the excess wheat was for consumption on his dairy farm, not for sale to a party in another state. All of Filburn's wheat began and ended its life in Ohio, all twenty-three acres of it.

Filburn correctly argued and the Court found that "the Act was not a permissible regulation of interstate commerce," but a federal law that addressed the "production and consumption of wheat." Filburn claimed that these were purely local activities that did not fall under the Commerce Clause.

The Court agreed with Filburn that he had engaged in a purely intrastate activity. However, it invented a new rationale which stated that it was permissible for Congress to regulate purely intrastate activity if the effects of similarly situated activities "*upon interstate commerce* were such as to make them a proper subject of federal regulation." In other words, if everyone grew wheat in their backyard then this would have a "substantial effect on interstate commerce." Even though Filburn's wheat in fact had *no* discernable effect on interstate commerce, the Court held that Congress could still regulate it.

In the opinion of the Court, Congress's power "extends to those intrastate activities which [when added to other similar activities] in a substantial way [may] interfere with or obstruct the exercise of the granted power." The Court conceded that "there is no decision of this Court that such activities may be regulated where no part of the product is intended for interstate commerce or intermingled with the subjects thereof." So what sort of tortured logic was the Court using?

Merely classifying something as "production" does not control whether Congress can validly regulate it. But the Court held that Congress could properly regulate the business of wheat within the states. There was a crisis in the wheat industry because of "increased foreign production and import restrictions" that caused a sharp decline in the exporting of American wheat. So a crisis allows a change in the Constitution?

The Court reasoned that the home production of wheat by everyone who grew it in his backyard (assuming he actually did so) in the "aggregate" could have a substantial effect on interstate commerce. Therefore, it was proper for Congress to regulate the local production of wheat. A more appropriate response to the wheat crisis would have been to let the free market adjust to the increased supply. In America, the land of choice, farmers would soon produce less wheat if there were a low demand for it. The Court noted that "exporting countries . . . have all undertaken various programs for the relief of growers," and thereby upheld President Roosevelt's socialist system.

What does Roscoe Filburn producing wheat for his own consumption have to do with interstate commerce? Nothing; it was just a power-grab by the feds.

After *Wickard*, it is hard to imagine an activity that Congress could not regulate. The Supreme Court had essentially repealed the system of enumerated powers on which the system of checks and balances is based. The onslaught arguably continued unabated until the Rehnquist Court's 1995 decision in *Lopez*. However, *Lopez* did not mark the end of the Court's use of *Wickard* as precedent.

REEFER MADNESS

Believe it or not, the Court invoked *Wickard* as recently as 2004, in *Gonzalez v. Raich* (2004), the case of Angel Raich and Diane Monson, two chronically ill women who suffered debilitating pain, such that their physicians prescribed medical marijuana to relieve pain.

Both patients were residents of California, where Proposition 215 (the Compassionate Use Act) authorizing the use of medical marijuana was passed by a 1996 referendum. However, that act arguably conflicts with the federal Controlled Substances Act of 1970, which outlaws the "manufacture, distribution, and possession of marijuana," making no exceptions for medical use.

In 2002, the feds entered Monson's home to seize and destroy her six marijuana plants. Monson and Raich filed suit seeking "to prohibit the enforcement of the federal Controlled Substances Act."

In arguing the case, the government blew smoke about *Wickard*, and the Court inhaled. The Court said, "As we stated in *Wickard*, 'even if appellee's activity be local and though it may not be regarded as commerce, it may still, whatever its nature, be reached by Congress if it exerts a substantial economic effect on interstate commerce.'" Writing for the majority, Justice John Paul Stevens wrote, "When Congress decides that the 'total incidence' of a practice poses a threat to a national market, it may regulate the entire class."

Last time I checked, Justice Stevens, there was no "legal" national market for marijuana!

Justice Stevens was quite emphatic about the similarities between *Wickard* and *Raich*. Key among them is Congress's "rational" basis for enacting the regulatory act.

Again, what is Congress regulating aside from someone's personal behavior?

Stevens continues: "In *Wickard*, we had no difficulty concluding that Congress had a rational basis for believing that, when viewed in the aggregate, leaving home-consumed wheat outside the regulatory scheme would have a substantial influence on price and market conditions."

The Court concluded, "Here too, Congress had a rational basis for concluding that leaving home-consumed marijuana outside federal control would similarly affect price and market conditions." Now, just where is the local marijuana store? What are the prevailing, congressionally regulable prices and market conditioners?

When Raich argued that Congress provided no evidence that medical marijuana had any effect on the market in the way that *Wickard* did when arguing about the effect of home consumed wheat on the market for wheat, Justice Stevens dismissed "evidence" as unnecessary. He said that Congress has never been required to provide such evidence. I think Congress should need only look to the Constitution to see what it can and cannot regulate!

The Court did not even address the factors that it introduced in *Lopez*. The dissent notes that "Today's decision allows Congress to regulate intrastate activity without check. . . ."

This is indistinguishable from the historical reading of *Wickard*. *Wickard* must die. It is a precedent that allows the heavy hand of government to do whatever it wants. It is not just about commerce. As we will see with other examples of our own federal government in wartime, we cannot afford to let the little things like regulations of wheat slide because eventually we will slide into much more serious situations. Justice Clarence Thomas wrote an eloquent dissent, which in one paragraph blew away the majority's position:

> Diane Monson and Angel Raich use marijuana that has never been bought or sold, that has never crossed state lines, and that

> has no demonstrable effect on the national market for marijuana. If Congress can regulate this under the Commerce Clause, then it can regulate virtually anything—and the Federal Government is no longer one of limited and enumerated powers. . . . By holding that Congress may regulate activity that is neither interstate nor commerce under the Commerce Clause, the Court abandons any attempt to enforce the Constitution's limits on federal power.[1]

In "50 Questions on the Natural Law," Professor Rice quotes German Judge Theodor Seidel: "Not everything that is legal is right," and "at the end of the 20th century, no one has the right to turn off his conscience when it comes to . . . the orders of the authorities." Rice goes on to state, "In the natural law tradition, law involves the will of the lawgiver who ordains and promulgates it, but the essence of law is reason."

In essence, if you give the government an inch, it will take a yard. It is a self-serving machine that, when given too much power, may use it for good, but, as history has proven, often turns on its own people.

12

HOW GENERAL IS YOUR WELFARE?

As you could guess by now, the "general welfare" these days has come to mean anything that Congress wants it to mean.

The General Welfare Clause in the Constitution says that the Congress may "provide for the common Defense and the general Welfare of the United States." Strict constructionists rightly believe that Congress can only legislate for the "general welfare" when it is tied to one of the eighteen enumerated powers. Yet collectivists, do-gooders, busybodies, and Big Government Republicans and Democrats don't seem to understand the concept.

The conflict as to how to interpret the phrase "general welfare" predates constitutional cases on the issue. Historical writings of the Founders, preeminent statesmen, and other politicians suggest a disparate approach that would later be distilled into the three views on the meaning of the General Welfare Clause.

The Hamiltonian interpretation claims an independent grant of power in the clause. This theory argues that Congress can enact any law in furtherance of the general welfare of persons in the United States. The Madisonian interpretation limits the congressional power to spend and to enact laws pursuant to the enumerated powers.

The Justice Joseph Story interpretation grants Congress the power *to spend* in furtherance of the general welfare. This theory differs from the Hamiltonian interpretation in that it does not authorize Congress to "enact any law"; rather it is limited to spending power.

Before assessing the historical meaning of the General Welfare Clause, we need to remember that the power to tax has evolved historically as well. While the power to tax conferred in the first portion of the constitutional provision is generally uncontroversial, it sheds some light on the intentions of the Founders with regard to the latter half of the provision, i.e., the General Welfare Clause.

According to scholar Jeffrey Renz, the power to tax was distinct from the power to raise revenue at the time when the wording of the clause was contemplated. The power to tax was the power to regulate trade. The power to regulate trade was acceptable to the colonies because the "duties were always imposed with design to restrain the commerce of one part, that was injurious to another, and thus to *promote the general welfare.*"[1]

To the Founders, the term "general welfare" was applied in connection with the regulation of trade. The colonists conceded that Parliament had the right to regulate trade because the power to regulate relations among the colonies, England, and foreign countries "establishes the basis of the British power; and from such a firm connection between the Mother Country and her Colonies, as will produce all the advantages she ought to wish for."[2]

However, the colonists protested Britain's attempts to seek revenue from the colonies. Britain periodically sought financial support from them, and colonial legislatures voted supplies to the Crown at their own discretion.

After the war with France, Britain attempted to collect revenue using taxation for the first time by enacting the Stamp Act in 1764.

Records from the period indicate that the colonists protested Parliament's power to tax for revenue without their consent. The Continental Congress thus passed the Resolutions of the Stamp Act stating that England could not tax citizens of the colonies without their consent. They argued against it "as a matter of right," and distinguished it from Parliament's power to regulate trade. Parliament had the right to regulate trade and commerce by taxation, but the colonists protested taxation for any other reasons.

After the Stamp Act was repealed, Parliament tried again with the Townshend duties, which were also enacted for the purpose of raising revenue. The colonists rejected paying the duties. The Contintinental Congress consented to Parliament's regulation of commerce, but resisted the imposition of taxes to raise revenue.

The Founders' understanding of the distinction between duties levied for revenue and those levied for regulation of trade persisted until the framing of the Constitution and, specifically, the General Welfare Clause.

With this understanding in mind—that the ability to levy taxes for the purpose of raising revenue is distinct from the ability to levy taxes for the purpose of regulating trade—we come to the conclusion that the General Welfare Clause limits rather than expands Congress's power.

WE'LL SPEND, YOU REGULATE

The Founders' understanding of how the General Welfare Clause should function was as disparate as the interests represented at the convention.

Robert Yates, who attended the Philadelphia Convention, interpreted the clause as granting Congress either unlimited power to tax and spend, or an unlimited power to legislate. Another attendee,

Oliver Elsworth, interpreted the clause as making void any use of the taxing power but for the purpose of paying debts and providing for defense. Abraham Baldwin, another delegate, proposed that this was the correct interpretation.

Between these delegates, whose interpretation should we treat as accurate? They were not debating the meaning of the clause at the time when these statements were made. They were documenting it, explaining it to others.

What the General Welfare Clause meant was a point of contention between the Federalists and Anti-Federalists. Thomas Jefferson articulated the different views of the two groups. He called the dispute "the only landmark which now divides the federalists from the republicans."

The Federalist doctrine, in 1817, was that the clause "was an extension of the powers specifically enumerated to whatever would promote the general welfare. . . ."

Jefferson was a proponent of the view that "Congress had not unlimited powers to provide for the general welfare, but were restrained to those specifically enumerated." As such, Congress was only empowered to spend "for the purpose of providing for the general welfare by the exercise of the enumerated powers."

Jefferson's letter to Albert Gallatin in 1817 said: "The act was founded, avowedly, on the principle that the phrase in the constitution which authorizes Congress 'to lay taxes, to pay the debts and provide for the general welfare,' was an extension of the powers specifically enumerated to whatever would promote the general welfare; . . . our tenet ever was . . . that Congress had not unlimited powers to provide for the general welfare, but were restrained to those specifically enumerated. . . ." Jefferson understood that the real meaning of the clause was a brake on Congress's spending. It could not raise a *private* army or build a *private* post office, or establish a *private* court system; it could not build a *private* road or a *private* house or office building, but rather only those from which all Americans—the general welfare—could benefit.

Hamilton believed that the Tax Clause granted Congress the power to tax, while the General Welfare Clause gave it the power to "enact any law in furtherance of the general welfare of the United States." The power to tax and spend was subject only to the limitation that it could not violate another constitutional provision.

The history of the provision suggests that Hamilton, and at least two other delegates (Roger Sherman from Connecticut and Gunning Bedford Jr. from Delaware), proposed language containing a broad legislative grant of authority. Their requests seem to have been denied, as the Convention did not adopt any of their particular suggestions.

The provision started with a limited proposal by Edmund Randolph that Congress should have the power to legislate "in all cases to which the separate states are incompetent." General Charles Pinckney proposed adding the power to "lay and collect taxes, duties, and other excises." Hamilton proposed instead that Congress should have power "to pass all laws which they shall judge necessary to the common defense and general welfare of the Union." There were other proposals, but when the committee presented the article, it had enumerated powers but omitted the power to pay debts, so the grant was not plenary.[3]

Henry St. George Tucker remarked that the Federalists attempted six times to insert a grant of general legislative power in the Constitution, without success. What's more, the version that was finally adopted had a comma where previous drafts indicated a semicolon that would have conferred an independent grant of authority. You could say that Hamilton's position is without punctuation.

The text of the Constitution itself also presents a problem with

Hamilton's interpretation. Madison later questioned why, if Congress intended to create an independent grant of authority with the General Welfare Clause, it would have taken the trouble to enumerate powers right after the supposed grant. The answer to the question is obvious: the clause is not an independent grant of power.

Justice Story would also later use the canons of statutory construction and interpretation to invalidate the Hamiltonian view. However, his view of giving Congress broad power was followed by Congress and the courts for many years.

Madison believed that the General Welfare Clause did not grant Congress any power to legislate, and only granted Congress the power to spend in furtherance of the enumerated powers contained in the article. In *Federalist* 41 he wrote that those who rejected the General Welfare Clause on the belief that it gave the government unlimited power were misrepresenting the provision in order to defeat it.

Madison wondered, "For what purpose could the enumeration of particular power be inserted, if these and all others were meant to be included in the preceding general power? Nothing is more natural nor common than first to use a general phrase and then to explain and qualify it by a recital of particulars." The history of the clause suggests Madison's view was justifiable.

There had been some discussion during the 1787 Philadelphia Convention that the new government should reassure people to whom the old government owed money. The old government was the one that existed under the Articles of Confederation. It was also proposed that the new government should assume the debts that had been created from the Revolutionary War.

At the Philadelphia Convention, General Livingston had proposed that Congress should be empowered to satisfy the debts of the

United States and assume those of the several states that were incurred "for the common defense and general welfare." The power to tax for this purpose was added to Livingston's language. The clause went through various changes, and it was proposed that it should cover debts that would be incurred for the common defense and general welfare. It was changed after that. But it is clear that the General Welfare Clause evolved from a discussion of settling common debts from the war. This idea was merged with the power to levy taxes, again, one could presume, for that purpose. Because the common defense and general welfare could encompass more than war debt, the language was made somewhat broad.

Madison recognized that the power was to be limited to particular objects. However, naming those objects might disadvantage the Congress in times of need. As he aptly noted, "money cannot be applied to the general welfare" unless it is applied to "some particular measure [in the enumerated powers], conducive to the general welfare." When money is raised for the general welfare, it cannot be applied to a measure over which Congress has no authority, thus "a question arises whether the particular measure be within the enumerated authorities vested in Congress."

Justice Story's view, articulated in his *Commentaries,* is that the General Welfare Clause is in fact a separate source of power, but is limited to spending for the general welfare, rather than being a grant to regulate for the general welfare as Hamilton argued. Thus it is a limit on the overall power to tax.

That means that Congress is empowered to apply the revenue to whatever the general welfare is, even if the object of the revenue is not something that Congress has authority over from the enumerated powers. Under this theory, Congress is also fully empowered to determine what the general welfare is.

Story reached this conclusion by reading the text. There were two possible interpretations, according to Story. The first would divide the entire clause into two separate clauses. The Tax Clause would operate separately, indicating that Congress was authorized to levy taxes, while the General Welfare Clause was a separate grant of power. He immediately dismissed this interpretation because it yields an absurd result. Taken this way, the clause grants Congress unlimited power in spite of the Constitution's specific and limited grants of power. This would make the government one of unlimited power despite the fact that none of the Founders understood it that way.

Story notes that a cardinal rule in statutory interpretation is that enumeration weakens the law in cases not enumerated. "Just as an exception strengthens the force of a law in cases not excepted, so enumeration weakens it in cases not enumerated." There would be no point to the enumeration if it was already encompassed in the general power. Thus the enumerated powers do not add anything to the general power. However, they are also not exceptions. So what would be the point of including them? Story says that if this were the appropriate construction of the clause, then the enumerations are either confounding, misleading, or absurd. It would charge the authors with "premeditated folly, or premeditated fraud."

It is quite natural, Story says, to state a broad proposition and then restrict it with a list of particular limitations. This is the second possible reading of the clause, and it is the one that Story says we must naturally arrive at. The General Welfare Clause is to be taken together with the Tax Clause, giving meaning to the whole phrase. The General Welfare Clause qualifies the Tax Clause as an "expression of the ends and purposes to be effected by the preceding power of taxation."

So who's right? The Hamiltonians, the Jeffersonians, or Justice

Story? Let's see how the General Welfare Clause has been used by Congress and the courts.

THE TRIPLE A

In 1933, Congress enacted the Agricultural Adjustment Act. It identified an economic emergency caused by the "disparity between the prices of agricultural and other commodities, with consequent destruction of farmers' purchasing power and breakdown in orderly exchange."

This, it was argued, had affected commerce in agricultural products to the extent that it had become a national public interest. As such, Congress sought to keep the "balance between production and consumption of agricultural commodities" in such a way as would reestablish prices and fix the industry so that a farmer's purchasing power would be the same as it was in the 1909 to 1914 time frame.

The act provided for two taxes to be levied in order to "obtain revenue for the extraordinary expenses incurred by reason of the national economic emergency."[4] One was a processing tax, and the other was a floor tax. The Hoosac Mills Corporation was presented with a claim for processing and floor taxes on the cotton that it produced, and it took both of these to court.

The act created the Agricultural Adjustment Administration, which was authorized to pay farmers not to produce certain crops and livestock, make advance payments to farmers, and collect processing taxes to pay for these activities. The Commodity Credit Corporation was created to carry out financial activities such as loans under the act.

The *Hoosac Mills* decision in 1936 declared unconstitutional the controls on production and processing taxes that had been collected under the Agricultural Adjustment Act of 1933. Congress was unhappy with this result, and in response it passed several laws to get around this decision. These laws include the Agricultural Adjustment Act of 1938, the Agricultural Marketing Act of 1937, and the Soil Conservation and Domestic Allotment Act of 1936. All of these are still valid law today.

According to the government, Congress passed the Agricultural Adjustment Act for the purpose of meeting emergencies that arose during the Great Depression. (The AAA was also the act at issue in *Wickard.*)

The act gave the secretary of agriculture authority to reduce acreage and production of any "basic agricultural commodity through agreements with producers or by other voluntary methods and to provide for rental and benefit payments in connection therewith. . . ."

The government embraced the Hamiltonian interpretation of the General Welfare Clause, arguing that it "should not be construed broadly to include anything conducive to the national welfare," yet "it is not limited by the subsequently enumerated powers."

This is an open rejection of the Madisonian view of the clause, and also a rejection of what is called the "strong" Hamiltonian view, i.e., that the clause gives Congress broad power to tax and legislate as it sees fit. However, this is an endorsement of Justice Story's position, also known as the "weak" Hamiltonian view. Unfortunately, the government could not cite other cases where this was discussed because this was the first time that the issue was in Court.

The Mills' lawyers made a compelling argument. They argued that the processing tax is really not a tax at all. Through some complicated mathematics, the government essentially determined what the ideal price of a crop should be and what the actual price is. The tax levied on processors was intended to cover the spread between the ideal price and the actual price. It was totally unrelated to the activity of the processors. It was intended to accomplish price regulation and wealth redistribution.

The Court reviewed the historical treatment of the General Welfare Clause. First, it said that the strong version of the Hamiltonian view—which would recognize a "power to provide for the general welfare independently of the taxing power"—had "never been authoritatively accepted."

However, the question of what constitutes the general welfare was a contentious issue, and the Court declared that Justice Story's reading of the clause would be the one adopted by the Court. The ability to spend and tax is therefore wider than the "direct grants of legislative power found in the Constitution."

In deciding which construction to adopt, Justice Roberts noted that this was the Court's first time addressing the issue. He said that the Court had "noted that question, but has never found it necessary to decide which is the true construction." He was unequivocal in his choice of Story's interpretation, going so far as to say that the "reading advocated by Mr. Justice Story is the correct one." The Court concluded that the act invaded rights reserved to the states in so far as it levied a tax on agricultural production.

Note that the Court seemed to be saying that with respect to general welfare, production is a right reserved to the states, but in *Wickard* it said that with respect to interstate commerce, production is subject to federal regulation. The Court at least respected some boundaries at this point in constitutional history.

The characterization of the exaction as a tax seems irrelevant, as it is but a means to an unconstitutional end. What the Court did was to say that there are inappropriate objects of appropriation, and this was one of them. The General Welfare Clause could not be invoked because this was a local issue. To rule otherwise would be to violate the Tenth Amendment.

The Court clearly distinguished between the use of the taxing power to accomplish constitutional ends, and the use of the power to achieve illegitimate objectives. While Congress has broad power to use various means in the exercise of its authority, it cannot "pass laws for the accomplishment of objects not entrusted to the Federal Government." The taxing power may not be used to "effectuate an end which is not legitimate."

THE DAILY DOUBLE

Two cases involving the General Welfare Clause, decided on the same day, *Steward Machine* and *Helvering,* confirmed the power of Congress to spend and tax. Both involved challenges to the Social Security Act of 1935, which the Court upheld.

Steward Machine Corp. challenged the constitutionality of the Social Security Act, particularly the Unemployment Compensation section. This law required companies employing at least eight people to pay an annual tax of a percentage of the total amount it paid in wages during the year. Congress was bold enough to call this tax an "excise tax"! Steward Machine paid the tax but claimed that it was unconstitutional. The company was correct. The Founders never would have permitted such a tax.

Can you imagine the Continental Congress allowing the British to tax the colonists and "save" the money until their retirement?

Steward Machine argued that the payments required under the act were not actually taxes and did not fall under the General Welfare Clause. Employment is a fundamental liberty, it argued, and as such it could not be burdened with taxes to support federal government programs. Steward Machine claimed that the government had no precedent for taxing fundamental rights.

Writing for the majority of the Court, Justice Cardozo rejected Steward Machine's arguments. As seen in the *Slaughterhouse* cases, the state and federal government can regulate where work is performed and charge fees in the form of taxes on work that is done. The Court said this does not constitute involuntary servitude in violation of the Thirteenth Amendment. Also, this is not a denial of the ability to work in violation of the privileges and immunities clause of the Fourteenth Amendment. Therefore, the act was constitutional.

Because unemployment was a serious problem for both the states and the federal government, "moneys of the Nation may be used to relieve the unemployed and their dependents in economic depressions and to guard against such disasters."

Helvering v. Davis concerned the section of the Social Security Act that collected taxes to pay benefits to older workers. A shareholder of Edison Electric Illuminating Company challenged the act. The shareholder sought to enjoin the company from paying the taxes required by the Social Security Act. The Court upheld the act and said the benefits to older workers provided for the general welfare.

Try to imagine James Madison thinking a centralized government would do better with his money than he could!

The Court affirmed its decision in *United States v. Butler* by rejecting Justice Story and stating that the federal government can constitutionally spend for the general welfare. *Butler* concerned a constitutional challenge to the Agricultural Adjustment Act of 1933, enacted by Congress to provide relief to farmers in economic crisis. The act set up a system of providing payments to the farmers in return for their agreements to limit their production of crops, livestock, and dairy products. These payments were a result of a tax imposed on processors; the tax money was sent directly from the processors to the farmers. Butler, a processor, refused to pay the tax and challenged the statute on the grounds that it is illegal for the government to use taxation to transfer wealth from one person to another. The majority of the Supreme Court agreed and held the act unconstitutional.

The *Helvering* Court had also rejected Justice Story's position and stated that the federal government can constitutionally spend for the general welfare. The Court disingenuously claimed that it agreed with Justice Story's interpretation of the General Welfare Clause: "The conception of the spending power advocated by Hamilton and strongly reinforced by Story has prevailed over that of Madison, which has not been lacking in adherents."

The Court even went as far as claiming that there is a "penumbra" around the General Welfare Clause, and Congress can better determine what needs to be regulated than the judicial branch. This is upsetting to the balance of power between the branches of the government. The Court seemed to indicate that the General Welfare Clause is designed to change as the legislative branch sees fit.

The Court pointed to several studies and statistics that indicated employment of older workers was an issue with national effects. It is interesting to note that the Court took it upon itself to look at economic data rather than the Constitution.

The Court tried to justify its decision by saying, "A system of old age pensions has special dangers of its own, if put in force in one state and rejected in another. . . . Only a power that is national can serve the interests of all."

The Court claimed that it only considered whether the provision was constitutional and did not examine its merits. The Supreme Court essentially granted Congress the ability to determine what falls under the General Welfare Clause. It wrote, "When money is spent to promote the general welfare, the concept of welfare or the opposite is shaped by Congress, not the states."

Why would the Court consider what Justice Story thought about the General Welfare Clause but ignore the opinion of the Founders?

If Congress can spend for the general welfare, it can spend for anything, even bribes, as we shall see.

Congress quickly realized that it could use federal funds to bribe states into complying with its wishes. Congress lacked the power to impose a national drinking age, but instead it conditioned the receipt of a portion of federal highway funds to states on enforcing a drinking age of twenty-one. When South Dakota objected to this policy, the Supreme Court upheld this coercion by Congress.

In *South Dakota v. Dole* (1987), the Court said that as long as the amount of money at stake is a relatively small portion of the total funds received under a program, Congress can condition the receipt of those federal funds on complying with its extra-constitutional wishes. Essentially, the Court held that as long as a bribe is not too large then it is valid!

Is this how the Founders envisioned Congress spending money for the "general welfare"?

Wait. It gets worse.

13

GREASING THE GOVERNMENT SKIDS

How Congress Bribes the States

Does Congress really bribe the states? You bet, and it's been doing so for some time.

In 1916, Congress enacted the Federal Aid Highway Act. It provided federal money to states for maintenance of their highways. In 1973, Congress enacted the Emergency Highway Energy Conservation Act as an amendment to the Federal Highway Act. It grants federal funds to the states on the condition that they impose a maximum speed limit of 55 mph on all highways, including secondary roads that are not part of the interstate network. The act was passed in response to the concern over the energy crisis that emerged in the early 1970s.

In 1985, Nevada passed a law that increased its speed limit to 70 mph. The law also provided that if the federal officials threatened to cut off aid to the state, the limit was to be lowered. Within sixty seconds of the new law coming into effect, the Chief of the Nevada division of the Federal Highway Administration advised that the federal Department of Transportation declared that all future funds for state highways would be withheld unless the Nevada speed limit was reduced to 55 mph.

Though the federal government amended the Highway Act to provide for an increase to 65 mph in low population density areas, Nevada filed suit because the new provision still clashed with its desired 70 mph limit. Nevada argued that because the Highway Act would cut 95 percent of its federal highway funding, the limit violated the "coercion" limitation on the federal spending power.

The federal trial court ruled in favor of the United States on this issue, and the U.S. Court of Appeals affirmed. Judge Stephen Reinhardt, writing for the Ninth Circuit Court of Appeals, found that a national speed limit was "rationally related" to the goals of Congress under the Highway Act, mainly lower consumption of gasoline. This goal was within the power of the Commerce Clause, so Congress could enact a national speed limit by coercing states with federal funds. Judge Reinhardt dismissed the argument that the federal government's conduct was overly coercive and held that the national speed limit was a valid exercise of the spending power.

Clearly, Judge Reinhardt was not bothered by the fact that Congress was attempting to bribe the states into doing something indirectly that it could not regulate directly. In several other cases the Supreme Court has held that pursuant to Congress's authority to tax and spend under Article I, Congress may condition the acceptance of funding on compliance with Congress's wishes in areas where *even Congress concedes that it is powerless to regulate* under the Constitution.

However, the Supreme Court has also articulated limits on the spending power: "1) Spending must be in pursuit of the general welfare; 2) the condition on receipt of federal funds must be reasonably related to the articulated goal; 3) Congress's intent to condition funds on a particular action must be authoritative and unambiguous, enabling the States to exercise their choice knowingly, cognizant of the consequences of their participation; and 4) the power may not be used to induce a state to engage in activities that would themselves be unconstitutional." These limits have "been much discussed but infrequently applied in federal case law, and never in favor of the challenging party." Part of the reason is that the word "coercion" is ill-defined. The Ninth Circuit ultimately did not reach a conclusion regarding the spending power, because it held that the government would have been well within its right to establish a national speed limit under the Commerce Clause.

Thus the Circuit Court avoided ruling on the heavy-handed use of the spending power, because under an enumerated power, commerce, Congress could validly force the states to conform to its regulations. Nevada argued that, under the Tenth Amendment, the state speed limit is a zone in which the commerce power may not intrude. The Court, not surprisingly, rejected the argument. Query: Has the Ninth Circuit invented a new basis upon which Congress can regulate traffic?

DRINK UP WHILE YOU CAN!

Congress passed the National Minimum Drinking Age of 1984 in response to political pressure claiming that varied legal ages at which people could consume alcohol resulted in teenagers traveling interstate to avoid states with stricter laws. The statute permitted the secretary of transportation to deny federal highway money to states with a minimum drinking age lower than twenty-one years.

South Dakota's minimum drinking age was nineteen in 1987. A nineteen-year-old was permitted to purchase liquor containing up to 3 percent alcohol. South Dakota filed suit in federal court seeking a judgment on the grounds that the enactment was an invalid "exercise of Congress's power under the spending clause" (in addition to a violation of the Twenty-First Amendment, which reserves power to the states to impose restrictions on the sale of liquor).

When the case reached the Supreme Court, Justices Powell, Marshall, White, Blackmun, Scalia, and Stevens joined in the Court's opinion written by Chief Justice Rehnquist. The Court said that while Congress may have lacked the ability to enforce a nationwide minimum drinking age, the enactment conditioning the federal funds on the state's drinking age was a valid exercise of Congress's spending power.

They arrived at this conclusion because the provision was created to further the "general welfare" alone. Paraphrasing Chief Justice Rehnquist, "the means chosen were reasonably calculated to advance the general welfare; the conditions upon which the states were to receive the funds were clearly stated; the congressional action was related to the national concern of safe interstate travel, one of the main purposes for which highway funds are spent, and the Twenty-First Amendment [ending Prohibition] did not provide an 'independent constitutional bar' to the enactment, since the statute did not induce the states to engage in unconstitutional activities and the percentage of funds withheld was relatively small." Thus, the Court found, there was no coercion.

Justices Brennan and O'Connor dissented separately. Justice Brennan dissented because he believed that the states had power under the Twenty-First Amendment to regulate the minimum liquor age, and that the act, because it abridged that right, was in conflict with the Constitution. Justice O'Connor dissented because "the establishment of a national minimum drinking age was not sufficiently related to interstate highway *construction* to justify so conditioning funds." Additionally, she held, the Twenty-First Amendment precluded it.

The Court disposed of the Twenty-First Amendment arguments

early in the opinion, suggesting that it need not decide that issue because under its spending power, Congress has authority to promote a uniform minimum drinking age across the states. The Court said this is permissible, though the Congress was doing indirectly what it could not do directly. The Court noted that "[W]e find this legislative effort within constitutional bounds even if Congress may not regulate drinking ages directly."

That is the core of the issue of Congress bribing the states. Congress is empowered under the Constitution to tax and spend, but the Court has found that "incident to this power, Congress may attach conditions on the receipt of federal funds."

The Court, in fact, made up a new rule in considering this issue. The chief justice wrote, "the constitutional limitations on Congress when exercising its spending power are less exacting than those on its authority to regulate directly."

In *Oklahoma v. Civil Service Commission*, a 1947 case, the Court had held that a "Tenth Amendment limitation on congressional regulation of state affairs did not concomitantly limit the range of conditions legitimately placed on federal *grants*."

So Congress, whose members have sworn to uphold the Constitution, and the Supreme Court, whose justices have taken the same oath, have at last colluded to permit congressional regulation of areas of human behavior nowhere even hinted at among Congress's eighteen specific, enumerated, delegated powers in the Constitution, so long as Congress pays for it! I guess it is easy to forget when one cashes a federal payroll check: after all, Congress doesn't pay for anything, does it? Taxpayers do.

The Constitution allows Congress to "lay and collect Taxes, Duties, Imposts, and Excises, to pay the Debts and provide for the common Defense and general Welfare of the United States."[1] Congress can make receiving federal funds contingent on complying with certain conditions. It has also used this power make companies jump through federal statutory and administrative hoops to receive funds.[2]

In *MCI,* the Court said, "These cases establish that the 'independent constitutional bar' limitation on the spending power is not, as petitioner suggests, a prohibition on the indirect achievement of objectives which Congress is not empowered to achieve directly."[3]

This is bribery, pure and simple.

A federal bribery statute was passed in 1984. This law prohibits the direct bribery of any federal official. It also outlaws the bribing of private individuals who are working on federally funded projects.

You are probably thinking that if bribery of federal officials is illegal, then bribery by federal officials should be illegal. How can members of Congress bribe state officials? The point of the federal bribery statute is that they cannot! Yet conditioning the receipt of federal funds on complying with Congress's wishes is essentially bribery with a constitutional fig leaf.

CONGRESSIONAL BRIBERY FLOURISHES

Congress passed Megan's Law in 1996. This law directs local police departments to record the addresses of convicted sex offenders and notify people when a convicted sex offender moves into their neighborhood.

Megan's Law was passed by the federal government, but directs states to develop programs. Any state that fails to operate such a program in compliance with federal standards will face a 10 percent reduction in federal highway funds. Again, the law has good intentions behind it, but the coercion by the feds on the states is simply unconstitutional.

The Solomon Amendment, which Congress passed in 1996, allows the secretary of defense to cancel federal funding to any college that prohibits military recruiting on its campus. This Amendment creates problems for universities with antidiscrimination policies.

The military follows an ill-advised Clinton-era statute that denies admission to and expels from its ranks known homosexuals. Many universities are governed by state laws against discrimination that poignantly prohibit sexual orientation as a basis for governmental decision-making. Moreover, law schools accredited by the American Bar Association are also bound by the ABA's dictates that prohibit discrimination based on sexual orientation. Due to the Solomon Amendment, many universities may be forced to violate state law and to abandon their own antidiscrimination policies if they want to continue receiving federal funds.[4] The government has sued to enforce the Solomon Amendment and require schools to adopt the army's antigay viewpoint. The Supreme Court will rule on the issue this year.

Congress has made federal funds for enforcing awards of child support available only to states that use computers or other automated procedures to process data and retrieve information. Several states did not comply with the federal requirements. Congress amended the law and reduced the penalties for noncompliance.

Congress has even sought to regulate access to pornography in public libraries. President Bush signed the Children's Internet Protection Act into law in 2001. This law makes the receipt of federal funds by public libraries contingent on them using computer software to filter pornography. This law broadly defines pornography to include "obscene" visual depictions, child pornography, and images "harmful to minors."

The American Library Association brought a lawsuit to challenge the constitutionality of the law in 2002. A federal trial court in Pennsylvania held that the law was unconstitutional, but the government appealed the case to the U.S. Supreme Court.

The Supreme Court found that the law was constitutional, reversing the lower Pennsylvania court. The Court said that the law did not violate the First Amendment. Enacting the law was a valid act by Congress, which was merely exercising its spending power.

Speaking of rank laws, *New York v. United States* (1992) concerned the disposal of radioactive waste. States were having trouble finding locations for radioactive waste dumps, so the federal government stepped in to create incentives for states to comply with the development of waste sites. The Supreme Court held that monetary "access incentives" allowing states to impose a surcharge on waste received from other states were valid.

The Court found that the "take title" provision that gave states a deadline for taking title (ownership) of the waste and finding sites to dispose of its waste—and made states liable for damages suffered by the waste's generator or owner—was unconstitutional. The "take title" provision went beyond a monetary incentive. It forced the states to take title to waste and assume liability for it. So the federal government was commandeering the decision-making power of the states.

The Court held that the "take title" provision violated the Tenth Amendment. Congress was commandeering the police power of the states.

That should not come as a shock. The federal government will take as much power as it can get away with. It is up to the Supreme Court to stop it and uphold the Constitution. Fortunately, the Court does not always let the federal government get away with blatant power grabs.

Printz v. United States (1997) concerned the federal government commandeering powers that are constitutionally left to the states. At issue was a provision of the Brady Handgun Violence Prevention Act (commonly known as the "Brady Bill"), which required chief law enforcement officers in local areas to perform background checks on anyone who attempted to buy a handgun.

Two county sheriffs challenged the provision. Congress claimed that under the Necessary and Proper Clause, Congress could temporarily require local law enforcement officers to perform background checks on handgun buyers.

The Supreme Court held that the federal government cannot give direct orders to state officials. Congress was unconstitutionally commandeering the power of the states when it forced local law enforcement personnel to comply with this provision of the Brady Bill. Justice Scalia, writing for the majority in *Printz*, stated the following:

> Residual state sovereignty was also implicit, of course, in the Constitution's conferral upon Congress of not all governmental powers, *but only discrete, enumerated ones.* Article I, Section 8, which [by] implication was rendered express by the Tenth Amendment's assertion that "[t]he powers not delegated to the United States by the Constitution, no prohibited by it to the States, are reserved to the States respectively, or to the people.

The Court noted that Congress can directly regulate commerce. However, as seen in *Lopez*, intrastate possession of a handgun or buying a gun that was produced in the state where the purchaser lives are not activities in interstate commerce. Therefore, Congress cannot directly pass laws affecting these activities under the Commerce Clause.

The Court said that the Necessary and Proper Clause does not allow Congress to force local officials to perform tasks on its behalf.

Congress does not only want to take discretion away from state and local officials. It also wants to tell them what to do!

14

BIG GOVERNMENT VERSUS INDIVIDUAL LIBERTY

Civil Liberties in Wartime throughout History

Prior to World War II, the nation was not very concerned with preserving civil liberties during times of war. In 1798, Congress enacted the Alien and Sedition Acts, which outlawed making maliciously false remarks regarding the president or the Congress.

The Alien and Sedition Acts of 1798 were passed during the presidency of John Adams, partially in response to the XYZ Affair in which France sent spies to the United States. Under the acts, the president could imprison any American citizen or deport any foreigner viewed as suspicious. The Acts even allowed the president to imprison certain aliens in the United States for as long as the president felt public safety required it.

These Acts were also used by the Federalists to attempt to stop the Democratic-Republican Party—also known as the Anti-Federalists—from growing.

In practice, the Alien and Sedition Acts of 1798 were rarely used. Only ten people were convicted under them, and just one alien was deported. By 1802, all of the Acts had either expired or been repealed. Jefferson—who opposed the Acts as violative of free speech—had let it be known he would veto any extension of them. The U.S. Supreme Court never actually ruled on the constitutionality of the Acts.

It was in response to Democratic-Republican criticisms of the Acts that the First Amendment was included in the Bill of Rights.

Recall from the Lincoln chapter the story of Clement L. Vallandigham. He was born in Ohio and was elected to Congress in 1858. As a congressman, Vallandigham was an outspoken advocate of states' rights. He was critical of Abraham Lincoln's handling the Civil War, and frequently expressed his views in public. Vallandigham was not reelected in 1862. In May 1863 he was arrested for *expressing sympathy* for the Confederacy. Lincoln apparently interpreted the First Amendment literally; he believed that it only prohibited *Congress* from abridging free speech.

Vallandigham was tried by a military tribunal for violating Lincoln's law and was convicted. Abraham Lincoln, not any federal court, upheld the conviction, and Vallandigham was exiled to the Confederacy.

THE DEATH OF *HABEAS CORPUS*

In 1863, Lincoln suspended *habeas corpus* in cases where the military wanted to try someone for an offense committed against the armed forces. Lambdin Milligan had allegedly been involved in Confederate activities in the state of Indiana. In 1864, he was tried by a military tribunal, convicted of supporting rebellion, and sentenced to death.

In *Ex parte Milligan*, the U.S. Supreme Court did not directly address the issue of the suspension of *habeas corpus.* The case concerned potential limitations on the imposition of martial law. The

United States was unquestionably at war during the time when Milligan was tried by a military tribunal. The question was whether the courts were functioning normally at the time and capable of hearing his case. At the heart of this issue is the power of the president to divert a prosecution from a federal district court to a military tribunal.

The Supreme Court held that the federal courts in Indiana had been functioning normally at the time Milligan faced a military tribunal. The Confederate army had not invaded Indiana. Because the federal courts were functioning uninterrupted, they had exclusive jurisdiction to try Milligan's case.

The Court held that neither the president nor Congress has authority to establish a military court to try civilians. Milligan was deprived of his constitutional right to a trial by jury. Because of this fact, his sentence was overturned and he was eventually set free.

Justice Davis, writing for the Court, noted that "The Constitution of the United States is a law for rulers and people, equally in war and in peace, and covers with the shield of its protection all classes of men, at all times, and under all circumstances."

It was fortunate for Milligan that his execution was scheduled for May 1865, which was, of course, after the formal end of the Civil War and Lincoln's death. If his execution had been scheduled for a date earlier than April 1865, Milligan would have been dead before the U.S. Supreme Court got a chance to hear his case and clarify the power of the president in wartime.

YOU SPY?

Following World War I, there were several "espionage" cases concerning civil liberties and national security. These cases were driven by wartime anxiety that worried more about perceived threats to national security than upholding constitutionally guaranteed civil liberties.

The Espionage Act of 1917, which was amended in 1918, was the first attempt by Congress to regulate speech since the Alien and Sedition Acts of 1798. The Espionage Act prohibited "conspiring, when the United States was at war with Germany, unlawfully to utter, print, write, and publish disloyal, scurrilous, and abusive language about the form of government of the United States, or language intended to bring the form of government of the United States into contempt, scorn, contumely and disrepute, or intended to incite, provoke, and encourage resistance to the United States in said war, or unlawfully and willfully, by utterance, writing, printing, and publication, to urge, incite, and advocate curtailment of production of things and products necessary and essential to the prosecution of the war."

Get that: *utter, print, write,* or *publish.* Did Congress believe it was subject to the First Amendment?

In *Abrams v. United States* (1919), the U.S. Supreme Court upheld the convictions of five Bolshevik sympathizers under the Espionage Act of 1917. The federal government claimed that the Espionage Act made it a criminal offense to *call for* the curtailment of military production with the intent to hinder the war with Germany.

The defendants had showered leaflets in English and Yiddish from a window of a manufacturing building upon the streets of New York City's lower east side. The leaflets denounced American intervention in the Russian Revolution and *called for* a general strike so as to prevent shipments of military hardware to the U.S. forces. One of the main charges against the defendants was that they conspired "when the United States was at war with the Imperial

German Government . . . by utterance, writing, printing and publication to urge, incite and advocate curtailment of production of . . . ordnance and ammunition, necessary and essential to the prosecution of the war."

The Supreme Court ruled that the convictions were proper, without being much concerned with the free speech interests involved. The Court developed here the "bad tendency" test, under which Congress can prohibit speech if it is of a type that would *tend* to bring about harmful results. The Court imputed to these defendants the knowledge that strikes in munitions factories would hinder any upcoming war effort, although at the time the leaflets were distributed, the United States was not in fact at war with Germany.

The dissent by Justice Oliver Wendell Holmes is far better reasoned, accords infinitely more fidelity to the Constitution, and has been cited exponentially more than the Court's majority opinion. Justice Holmes's dissent is probably his most frequently quoted dissent. It is principally remembered for its eloquent exposition of a philosophical foundation for the First Amendment: the government can only restrict freedom of expression when there is a clear and present danger of immediate evil as a consequence of the speech. The evil had to be so pressing and immediate as to preclude *time* for more speech to counter the offending expression. The use of words which on their face might, as the majority said, bring about harmful results, can never be the subject of a criminal prosecution if the speech is so ineffective that it is unlikely to achieve its intended goal.

Justice Holmes stressed that Congress cannot constitutionally make all antiwar speech illegal. He apparently believed that the actions of the defendants were of little consequence and presented an insignificant danger.

THE FIRST AMENDMENT SUSPENDED!

In *Gitlow v. New York* (1925), the Supreme Court upheld a conviction in a New York state court for violating a statute which prohibited the advocacy of criminal anarchy. The defendant published a didactic work called the "The Left Wing Manifesto." The Court found that the legislative determination of the inherent dangers of advocating anarchy is within the State's police power.

The New York Criminal Anarchy Law of 1902 criminalized any speech advocating the overthrow of the government. Benjamin Gitlow, a member of the Socialist Party, published and circulated two pamphlets written in English that advocated socialism and encouraged violent overthrow of the government if necessary. He was charged with criminal anarchy (otherwise known as freedom of speech), punishable by imprisonment, under the New York law.

Gitlow argued that his materials did not violate the statute and that the statute was an unconstitutional violation of the Fourteenth Amendment. He wanted the Court to rule that the Fourteenth Amendment's Due Process Clause effectively applied the First Amendment ("Congress shall make no law . . . abridging the freedom of speech") to the states. He was convicted in the lower court, and the decision was affirmed on appeal. The Supreme Court addressed only one question in the matter, "whether the statute, as construed and applied in this case by the state courts, deprived the defendant of his liberty of expression in violation of the due process clause of the Fourteenth Amendment." The Court found that the Fourteenth Amendment applied the freedom of expression portions of the First Amendment to the states, meaning that even though the First Amendment prohibits *Congress* from abridging speech, hereafter it would be interpreted as prohibiting *the states* form doing so as well. But this new jurisprudence was not enough to help Benjamin Gitlow.

The Court determined that First Amendment rights are guaranteed to citizens at the state level by operation of the liberty clause in the Fourteenth Amendment. However, the Court held, a state may forbid certain speech where the speech is *likely* to endanger the public. This was briefly known as the "dangerous tendency" test, and it provides a state legislature the freedom to determine that certain classes of speech should be prohibited because of the danger presented. A showing of actual harm resulting from the speech is not required.

The Court found Justice Holmes's clear and present danger test inapplicable here because only when a statute prohibits particular acts without including any restrictions on language should the clear and present danger standard be employed to determine if the particular speech could be constitutionally protected. But here the legislature had already determined what would violate the statute.

Justice Holmes and Justice Brandeis dissented. Without replying to the Court's distinction between a statute written without reference to speech and one aimed at speech as such, they found the clear and present danger test alone is both a safeguard for expressive liberties and an instrument through which the government can maintain order. The dissent said that where there is no likelihood of success, the speaker should be constitutionally free to make whatever utterances he chooses. All ideas must be given an equal chance to gain popular attraction.

Allowing the government to determine what is "dangerous" speech is exceptionally dangerous! The Founders did not place any limits in the text of the First Amendment. Having just been through the American Revolution, they were familiar with antiwar speeches and publications. It is clear that the Founders did not intend the result in *Gitlow.*

Then-governor of New York Al Smith pardoned Gitlow in 1925.

He acknowledged that Gitlow was a victim of a paranoid government during a time of war. But the courts should have known that war is no excuse for limiting freedom of speech, which is protected by the First Amendment.

9/11 MINUS EIGHTY YEARS

During the "Red Scare" following World War I, anarchists targeted prominent capitalists and government officials. They began sending mail bombs, many of which the government was able to intercept. Targets included J. P. Morgan, John D. Rockefeller, and Justice Holmes. Attorney General A. Mitchell Palmer (also a target) responded by creating a division within the Department of Justice to smoke out terrorists.

Between 1919 and 1921, the government conducted raids (orchestrated by Palmer and his young assistant, J. Edgar Hoover) of homes and schools, and detained resident aliens, some of whom were deported or incarcerated. About five thousand persons were rounded up in the raids. None was charged. Most were innocent. The government's claimed powers to arrest anarchists without charge and incarcerate them without trial are identical to President Bush's present-day claims that he can do likewise to "enemy combatants." The Supreme Court rejected that argument in an eight to one ruling in June 2004. This is an excellent example of what can happen to citizens when the federal government gets too powerful. Although the Red Scare victims were eventually released, they were not compensated for their lost time or the humiliation associated with their arrest and detention.

Despite enjoying strong public support initially, Palmer's credibility (and the zeal accompanying his anti-Red movement) waned significantly after he predicted terrorist attacks that never occurred.

He was accused of embezzling government funds and retired to obscurity.

"SAFETY" FIRST

After World War II, the courts heard several cases relating to the internment of Japanese Americans during the 1940s. Civil liberties had been greatly limited during World War II, even in the United States. In *Korematsu v. United States* (1944), the Supreme Court said that the protections guaranteed to all citizens under the Fourteenth Amendment could be curtailed in times of war when national security was in question.

In *Korematsu*, the U.S. military, in compliance with orders from President Roosevelt, promulgated the Civilian Exclusion Acts which prevented Japanese Americans from being in certain areas of the west coast. Fred Korematsu was an American citizen of Japanese heritage, born in California. He was convicted of being in one of the areas restricted under the acts. Korematsu argued that the danger presented by a Japanese invasion in the area was remote and that neither the Congress nor the military could curtail his freedom of movement without proof of personal criminal behavior on his part. He also argued that because the exclusion orders were based solely on race and ethnicity—the use of which by the government is prohibited by the Thirteenth and Fourteenth Amendments—they were invalid. The Court considered the protection offered by the Fourteenth Amendment, but said, "pressing public necessity may sometimes justify the existence of such restrictions. . . ."

The Supreme Court upheld the Civilian Exclusion Acts and Korematsu's conviction, citing *Hirabayashi* as precedent. *Hirabayashi* involved a curfew that was imposed on Japanese Americans. The Court upheld the curfew, even though it was applied against citizens of Japanese ancestry only. The Court said that the curfew was an "exercise of the power of the government to take steps necessary to prevent espionage and sabotage in an area threatened by Japanese attack." This is the same principle on which *Korematsu* was decided.

After World War II, the Supreme Court considered times of war to be special circumstances. The ends would justify the means when the United States was at war, particularly a large-scale war.

Regarding civil liberties during times of war, Justice Hugo Black, a former Klansman, wrote that "hardship is part of war, and war is an aggregation of hardships. . . . Citizenship has its responsibilities as well as its privileges, and in time of war the burden is always heavier."

Justice Frankfurter concurred in *Hirabayashi*, but noted that the Constitution specifically refers to war. Therefore, wars should be fought within the parameters set forth in the Constitution without a significant infringement upon the civil liberties of American citizens.

Justice Frankfurter indicated in *Hirabayashi* that even during wartime, the military must obey and respect the Constitution. Commenting on the power of the army during a war, he said, "To recognize that military orders are 'reasonably expedient military precautions' in time of war and yet to deny them constitutional legitimacy makes of the Constitution an instrument for dialectic subtleties not reasonably to be attributed to the hard-headed Founders. . . ."

Justice Roberts dissented in both cases. He said that "it is the case of convicting a citizen as a punishment for not submitting to imprisonment in a concentration camp, based on his ancestry, and solely because of his ancestry, without evidence or inquiry concerning his loyalty and good disposition towards the United States."

Justice Roberts equated the treatment of Japanese Americans with concentration camps in Europe.

Justice Murphy also dissented in *Korematsu.* He thought that the policy of excluding American citizens from certain areas based on their race was abhorrent, noting that civil liberties are too important to be trampled and ignored during wartime. Justice Murphy noted that any alleged safety concerns of the government "cannot be said to justify violations of constitutional rights of individuals."

From 1941 to 1946, the Supreme Court decided thirteen cases involving wartime offenses including sabotage, espionage, and treason. The government won only six of these cases. The Supreme Court seemed to "lean over backwards to avoid wartime penalties."[1]

IMPORTING PERSONS TO IMPRISON

Iva Toguri D'Aquino was an American citizen who was born and raised in California, U.S.A. In July 1941, she headed for Japan in order to take care of her sick aunt. Due to the error of a U.S. bureaucrat, she left without a passport and only with a "certificate of identification." When the Japanese attacked Pearl Harbor in December 1941, she was stranded in a foreign land without the proper paperwork from her own American government.

While stranded in Tokyo, she struggled to survive and became employed as a radio announcer for a propaganda program called "Zero Hour." She planned to quit her job and return to the United States when the war was over. She refused to renounce her American citizenship and never became a citizen of Japan.

While working as a radio announcer, Toguri met two prisoners of war from Australia and the United States. The POWs were being forced to write propaganda broadcast material in English that was designed to influence Allied servicemen. Toguri was forced to read the propaganda materials on the air, along with thirteen other female broadcasters. Covertly, these POWs were working to undermine the entire propaganda operation with the help of Toguri by sabotaging the anti-American rhetoric.

Still, despite these pro-American efforts, Iva Toguri D'Aquino was arrested after the war amidst a sea of anti-Japanese-American sentiment. Taken into U.S. custody in Japan, she was brought to the United States for trial in the famous "Tokyo Rose" case. During much of her detention, Toguri was denied counsel, denied visits from her family, and was even gawked at while bathing by American Congressmen.

The U.S. government alleged that she had delivered anti-American messages and top-secret information regarding the navy's warships in the course of her job as a radio announcer. In fact, there were fourteen women at the radio station where Toguri worked who broadcast propaganda aimed at American soldiers and sailors. The name "Tokyo Rose" was actually a generic term given by U.S. troops to any female voice on Japanese radio programs broadcast during World War II.

In his 1976 article, "The Framing of Tokyo Rose," historian James J. Martin summarizes the government's railroading of this innocent American scapegoat: "The striking thing about the vast efforts and expenditures of the prosecution was the miserable tidbit of material it used to send Mrs. D'Aquino to jail for ten years and fine her $10,000. Its vainglorious brandishing of 340 recordings, deflated to 18, then to 13, to 8, and finally to 6, was then pinched down to a mere 25 words allegedly uttered on a single broadcast."[2]

In other words, when levying charges and waging the press war against her, the prosecution claimed 340 recordings would prove her guilt; in the end, 339 recordings were dismissed. The government's whole case was based around 25 words in just one recording! The treasonous words she allegedly uttered? Here's the entire quip: "Now you fellows have lost all your ships. You are really orphans of the Pacific. How do think you are going to get home?"

Unbelievably, the only two witnesses to this supposed speech of Toguri's were Japanese nationals. As Dr. Martin so fittingly adds, "No one thought it strange that not a single U.S. citizen had presented evidence of treason that the court would accept."

To say the least, the charges were weak, but other key aspects of her trial left even more to be disturbed about. All of the jurors were Caucasian; not even one non-Caucasian in an era of American history when racial tensions boiled. So much for a jury of one's peers! To make matters worse, the judge should have removed himself from the case. He prejudicially lectured the jury on the government's expenses for the trial and the jury's need to come to a decision based on the price tag of the prosecution of Toguri. The behavior of the federal prosecutors was equally appalling. At one break in the trial, Ms. D'Aquino's defense counsel was preparing a Japanese witness for testimony in a public hallway of the federal courthouse in San Francisco at lunchtime. The witness was to testify for the defense after lunch. When prosecutors learned of this, they ordered FBI agents to kidnap the witness and forcibly put him on a plane to Tokyo. He landed in Japan the next day and never testified.

Remarkably, her conviction was for broadcasting information concerning the loss of U.S. Navy ships on an "unknown day" in October 1944. The government could not even list the day that she had supposedly done this! In addition, how could the U.S. government be so certain that it was Toguri who did this broadcast, considering that there were thirteen other female broadcasters at the radio station?

Amazingly still loyal to America, she stayed in the country after serving ten years in jail. About twenty-seven years after she was convicted, two witnesses who had testified against her admitted that they had been threatened by government prosecutors and forced to testify falsely. President Gerald Ford pardoned Toguri in 1977—the first time in American history that a presidential pardon was granted for a treason conviction.

As this case makes clear, the government does not care much for facts and true guilt when it is suppressing free expression during wartime. Perceptions and fears are enough to steamroll over constitutionally guaranteed liberties.

15

AFTER 9/11

Without question, America is different post 9/11. We live in a time of fear. Soon after the tragic events of that horrible day, the USA PATRIOT Act was quickly cobbled together. Unfortunately, in our fear, we allowed the final version of the act to pass despite the fact that it is directly and profoundly offensive to our Constitution.

In fact, the version of the act distributed to Congress did not even contain all the language of the act. Members of Congress voted on it without even reading it! Only a summary of the language was given to House members by the Justice Department until just moments before the vote. And only two senators—one of whom has since died—have ever publicly acknowledged reading the bill before it became law.

The PATRIOT Act and its progeny are the most abominable, unconstitutional governmental assaults on personal freedom since the Alien and Sedition Acts of 1798.[1]

In effect, the government says, "give us your freedoms, and we will protect you." Such a Faustian bargain misunderstands the nature of freedom and historically has never worked. After then-Attorney General A. Mitchell Palmer arrested without charge over 5,000 Eastern European intellectuals during World War I and after the United States interned more than 110,000 Japanese Americans during World War II, we looked back in horror at what was done.

But we have not learned. Since 9/11, hundreds, if not thousands, of Arab Americans have secretly disappeared from our streets. Sacrificing freedom has never made us safer, just less free. And the effects of this legislation will last.[2]

You see, by manipulating legitimate fears after a serious security crisis, the government can make changes that permanently erode liberties. Recently, the sunset clauses on the intrusive provisions of the PATRIOT Act were repealed by Congress, making them permanent features of our federal laws.

USA PATRIOT is an acronym used to refer to this bill, whose full name is the act to "Uniting and Strengthening America by Providing Appropriate Tools Required to Intercept and Obstruct Terrorism."

Rep. Diana DeGette, Democrat from Colorado and one of the few opponents of the bill, said, "in an end run around bipartisanship and the committee process, the House majority leadership brought a different and controversial bill to the floor without allowing time for committee consideration and without even giving Members time to figure out what the bill does."

Representative DeGette noted that the bill would "allow federal investigators to obtain search warrants without specifically naming each person who is involved . . . and allow federal authorities to obtain information like credit card numbers and bank account numbers with a subpoena, not a court order, as is the case under current law."

In former Attorney General John Ashcroft's testimony to the House Judiciary Committee (June 5, 2003), he said, "Congress overwhelmingly approved the USA PATRIOT Act. In the House, Representatives voted 357 to 66 for the measure, while the Senate supported the legislation by a near unanimous 98-to-1 vote. The PATRIOT Act gave us the tools we needed to integrate our law enforcement and intelligence capabilities to win the war on terror."

Even though the USA PATRIOT Act may help law enforcement personnel combat terrorism, it is doing so in a way that is giving more power to the federal government at the expense of the constitutionally guaranteed liberties of every person in America. Chances are, your congressman and senator voted for it without reading it and without thinking about the violence it implemented against the Constitution and your constitutional rights.

A HISTORICAL PERSPECTIVE?

When we were colonists, the British king and Parliament came up with ingenious ways to raise money. One of the ways that Parliament raised money was by enacting the Stamp Act, which required that every official piece of paper in the possession of colonists bear the king's stamp. An official piece of paper meant a book, a mortgage, a deed, a lease, and even a poster that one would nail to a tree.

How did the king go about collecting money under the Stamp Act? How did the king *know* if papers in one's private possession bore his stamp? Parliament enacted the Writs of Assistance Act, authorizing the issuance of open-ended search warrants, which allowed the king's soldiers *to give themselves permission* to knock on any door they wanted by writing for themselves permission to do so. The king's soldiers literally just wrote the warrant out, presented it to the colonists at the door, and demanded entrance to search for the stamps.

Like the government throughout all of history, they would find and look for all kinds of things above and beyond the stamps. They might ask, "Was this furniture imported from the islands? Did you pay a tax on it?" Alternatively, perhaps they would inquire, "This rum we found in your barn; where did you buy it? We didn't see a tax stamp on the bottle."

Because of such intrusions, we fought the Revolution, we won the Revolution, and we wrote a Constitution. Among other things, we prohibited in that Constitution self-written search warrants.

The Constitution was enacted because Thomas Jefferson and his Anti-Federalist colleagues agreed to support it only if a Bill of Rights was added. The fourth article of the Bill of Rights, known as the Fourth Amendment, prohibits unreasonable searches and seizures except upon a search warrant, issued by an impartial judge, after the judge is satisfied that there is probable cause of a crime or evidence of a crime on the property of the person to be searched.

Basically, the court must find that it is more likely than not that in the area to be searched or the person to be searched there will be evidence of a specific crime. The Fourth Amendment clearly prohibits search warrants from any authority other than a judge. This "right to privacy" as we call it is something that Americans enjoyed for 180 years until it began slowly to be attacked and worn away by the government.

The Fourth Amendment is uniquely American. It puts a neutral judge between the government, state or federal, and the government's domestic targets, no matter how odious the target.

In 1977, under the presidency of Jimmy Carter, the Congress enacted the Foreign Intelligence Surveillance Act (FISA). FISA established a super-secret court that would meet in a windowless room in a subbasement of the Justice Department. We would know the names of the judges on the court, but there would not be a stenographer present. Only the government can appear before the court.

This court would have the authority, for the first time in

American history, to issue search warrants on other than probable cause of a crime. The FISA statute allows the judges on this super-secret court to issue a search warrant on probable cause that the target of the warrant is an agent of a foreign government. So we have gone from probable cause of a crime to probable cause of status: the agent of a foreign government. It could be a friendly foreign government, like Great Britain or (at the time) West Germany, or it could be a hostile foreign government like the former Soviet Union. The person could be the ambassador or a janitor. He or she only had to be an agent of a foreign government.

Even Jimmy Carter insisted that whatever government agents found when they served these FISA warrants could not be used as evidence in a criminal trial. Why? Because the Fourth Amendment says the government can only get evidence from someone against his or her will when there is probable cause of a crime. So if the foreign janitor was found to be a spy who was beating his wife, he was not prosecuted for domestic violence or for espionage. Rather, he was kicked out of the country. FISA prohibited the use of evidence obtained from these search warrants in criminal cases.

In 1978, the Congress did FISA one better with the so-called Right to Financial Privacy Act. For the first time in American history, this act permitted something called a national security letter, which is government-speak for a self-written search warrant. It permits agents of the government—FBI agents, Treasury agents, Secret Service agents, and agents of some parts of the government that the government doesn't even acknowledge exist—*to write their own search warrants* and serve them on financial institutions. It still does not permit the use of evidence obtained from these self-written search warrants in criminal cases. Why? For the same reason as FISA: there was no judge, and thus there was no finding of probable cause as the Fourth Amendment requires.

In 1986, Congress enacted the Electronic Communications Privacy Act of 1986. Remember how in order to get a warrant from the FISA court you needed to show probable cause that the target was a foreign agent? The 1986 act changed foreign *agent* to foreign *person*. Therefore, the individual did not have to be an agent of a foreign government, but only a human being not native to the United States. Recall how the national security letters from the 1978 act could only apply to financial institutions? They could now apply to the digital as well as the hard copy records of financial institutions.

So follow the slippery slope thus far: for 177 years, if the government wanted something from you in the United States, and it followed the law, it went to a judge, federal or state, and presented evidence that it was more likely than not that you committed a crime or possessed evidence of a crime. If the judge agreed, a search warrant would be signed, but if the judge disagreed, the search warrant would not be signed. Then the law changed this for agents of foreign governments; then "foreign agents" to "foreigners." Next, the government went to financial institutions' hard paper copies, then to financial institutions' digital copies. President Reagan made the same demand as Jimmy Carter: no criminal prosecutions on the basis of whatever evidence is unearthed by these self-written search warrants because the Constitution prohibits it.

We all know what happened on 9/11. The magnitude of it is almost impossible to describe. Those of us who were in New York were perhaps more terrified than those in the rest of the country. And that fear could be harnessed.

Within thirty days of 9/11, President George W. Bush proposed the USA PATRIOT Act. The PATRIOT Act is the most unpatriotic of the things that the Bush administration and this Congress could have visited upon us. When then-Attorney General John Ashcroft advocated before the House Judiciary Committee, he said, in effect, "we need the powers under this PATRIOT Act. We need them so badly—there are so many bad people out there that we need to prosecute—that there isn't enough time to debate it."

Ask your members of Congress how much time they spent in debate on the PATRIOT Act in the House of Representatives and they will tell you—if they are honest—zero. Ask your member of Congress how much time he or she spent reading the PATRIOT Act before voting on it. The answer would again be "zero."

Unlike most members of Congress, I have actually read the PATRIOT Act. Reading such an act of law is not like reading a novel. Instead, it is a research mission. It requires that you have in front of you the full criminal code of the United States because the PATRIOT Act says things like, "in place of 'or' make it an 'and,' in place of that semi-colon make it a comma, in place of six months make it eight months." It is necessary for you to shuffle back through a lot of pages in other sources in order to understand the act's effects.

Only a few members of Congress threatened to reveal that they were not permitted debate. So the House agreed to a trigger provision. A trigger provision simply means if any member of Congress wants to debate the PATRIOT Act, after it is already law, the House will stop whatever it is doing and conduct the debate then and there—after, of course, the PATRIOT Act is law—to satisfy those House members who had the temerity to demand debate. So the PATRIOT Act was enacted with the trigger provision.

Now federal agents and local police can write their own search warrants, serve them on American financial institutions without the intervention of a judge, and obtain information about *you* without you even knowing it! Of course, the Carter reservation and the Reagan reservation about "no use in criminal prosecutions" are long gone.

Not only may the information obtained under self-written search warrants served under the PATRIOT Act be used in a criminal prosecution, but also the receivers of that information are now *required* to share it with law enforcement. The PATRIOT Act has allowed the government to circumvent completely the Fourth Amendment requirement of a search warrant in order to obtain information to be used against an individual in a criminal prosecution.

One might think that victims of such abuse might simply turn to the media and expose it. But the PATRIOT Act makes it a crime—punishable by five years in jail—for the recipient of a self-written search warrant to tell anyone that he or she has received the search warrant.

Before the PATRIOT Act, if the government wanted bank records it would go to a grand jury and present evidence of wrongdoing, or it would go to a federal judge and it would present evidence of probable cause. If the grand jury agreed or the federal judge agreed, and the subpoena from the grand jury or the search warrant from the federal judge were issued, it would be served on the bank and the bank would advise the person whose records the government sought of its intention to comply and of the date of compliance.

The person would then have time to go to a judge and challenge the subpoena or search warrant. Maybe the bank account number was wrong? Maybe it wasn't you they were after? Maybe the agents exaggerated or lied in the evidence they presented to the grand jury or the judge? Such appeals are no longer available under the PATRIOT Act.

The PATRIOT Act destroys the Fourth Amendment right to privacy and the First Amendment right to free speech. In a recent case in Bridgeport, Connecticut—we do not even know the name of the plaintiff who sued John Ashcroft (amended to Alberto Gonzales)—challenging this person's rights, not to keep the documents from the government, but to tell the world that the government wants the documents. The PATRIOT Act even makes it a crime for that person to go into court and tell a federal judge what the government did to him or her.

That's how inclusive the PATRIOT Act's prohibition on free speech is: thou shall not speak to thy spouse, child, neighbor, friend, lawyer, publisher, broadcaster, journalist, or even federal judge; so the Connecticut litigation is called *John Doe v. Alberto Gonzales.*

As if all of this is not enough, the federal government, in the PATRIOT Act, enacted a provision called "sneak and peak." The government can now, with an order from a judge, break into your house when you're at a basketball game on a Saturday afternoon, steal your checkbook, put an electronic bug under your kitchen table, and make it look like it was a house burglary. It can even leave and not tell you or the local police what has happened.

Can you imagine coming home on a Saturday night, finding out your house was broken into, your checkbook is missing, and it was the federal government that did it? This "sneak and peak" allows the government to withhold for up to six months that its agents were the thugs who perpetrated the break-in.

A self-written search warrant? They could write it on the back of a matchbook. Why make them write anything if they can write themselves permission to come into your house? Just let the government ransack the place! That is what the PATRIOT Act has made possible.

As if all of this were not enough, on December 13, 2003—the president signed the Intelligence Authorization Act for fiscal year 2004. Sounds like a harmless piece of litigation. Remember FISA? Remember the Electronic Privacy Act. Remember what their targets were? Financial institutions. Remember how FISA let the government get the records from a financial institution of a foreign person and the Electronic Surveillance Act let them get records from a financial institution?

This statute gives us a new definition of a financial institution. One would think that a financial institution would be a bank, a trust company, or a private bank. The Bush administration defined financial institution so as to include the following: a credit union, a stock broker, an investment banker, an insurance company, a pawn broker, an accountant, a hospital, an HMO, a computer server, a telephone company, a physician, a pharmacist, a delicatessen, a bodega, a travel agency, an automobile agency, a boat dealer, a real estate broker, a lawyer, and that great financial institution to which we would all repose our fortunes, the post office.

For the first time in American history, the government, without showing probable cause and without getting a search warrant from a judge, can read your mail before you do, can go to your lawyer's office and seize your files and the lawyer can't tell you, and it can do the same with a bank, with a hospital, with your physician, and with your pharmacist.

Remember where you were on December 13, 2003? Why would George W. Bush sign a piece of legislation on that day? Did something happen on that day that would keep his signature on this legislation off the front pages? Yes. It was the day we captured Saddam Hussein. The story about the legislation was buried.

This statute was not even made public until January 29, 2004, when an intern stumbled on it in the Code of Federal Regulations. As if all of this were not enough, Congress enacted, three months later, the Intelligence Reform Act of 2004, which permits the government to do the following: deport foreign-born persons without a charge and without a trial. You could be legally in the United States for decades, and the government can deport you without telling you why or giving you the opportunity to confront charges and resist.

When the government proceeds against you in a criminal case, it has the burden of proof. It has to come forward with evidence showing why you are bad. When you are arrested and you ask for bail, the government has to show why the defendant should not be permitted bail. This is no longer the case. Because if the government after you are arrested says you are a flight risk, you must prove that you are not. For the first time, the burden of proof has been set on its head, because before this statute, the burden of proof, the obligation of moving forward, was always on the government in a criminal case. Now, if the government says you are a flight risk, you must prove you are not a flight risk!

For example, everybody wants to know what is happening before the grand jury before which Karl Rove appeared. Grand juries operate in secret. For two hundred years, we respected that secrecy. The theory was, if the grand jury did not indict, then the public would never know that an innocent person was the subject of its investigation. For two hundred years, it was a violation of the federal rules of criminal procedure for anyone to leak information that came before a grand jury. Not anymore. The Intelligence Authorization Act permits federal prosecutors to leak what they learn before the grand jury.

Remember the PATRIOT Act trigger? Any member of the House sends a letter to the Speaker and the House will stop what it is doing and debate the PATRIOT Act even though it is three years old? The Intelligence Act abolished the trigger, before it was pulled.

16

THE PATRIOT ACT IS COMING

Let's face it. If you allow it, any unchecked government will steal your liberties. In times of peace, it enacts Nanny State legislation. In times of war, it sells its agenda as a bargain: a little liberty for a whole lot of perceived security. A government that can ignore the precepts and guarantees of the Constitution is a bad deal all around.

That great American poet Bruce Springsteen recently wrote that "Fear is a powerful thing, it'll take your God-filled soul and fill it with Devils and Dust." Fear grants Congress permission to rewrite our laws in order to catch the bad guys. Fear requires us to live with the changes that they've made once the threat is over. Fear makes us, the people, the target of Congress's illegitimate behavior. Fear blinds Congress to the Constitution. Fear lets the government justify anything.

The Bush administration does not take seriously its duty to uphold the Constitution and in fact looks for new ways to undermine basic constitutional liberties. The PATRIOT Act is being used in ways that Congress never intended. Sen. Harry Reid (D-Nevada) dryly remarked that "The law was intended for activities related to terrorism and not to naked women."

In a recent Nevada case, investigators used the PATRIOT Act to gather evidence from two stockbrokers allegedly involved in the corruption of a Las Vegas strip club owner. Federal agents assumed they could use self-written search warrants to obtain evidence, thereby by-passing the Constitution they swore to uphold.

The FBI used the PATRIOT Act to seize financial records from the owners of the strip club. Federal agents were looking for evidence of bribery and money laundering. The FBI was able to perform the search and seizure without first getting a search warrant approved by a judge.

In another bizarre case, Adam McGaughey, the Web master of a site for fans of the television show "Stargate SG-1," was accused of computer fraud and copyright infringement. The FBI used self-written search warrants authorized by the PATRIOT Act to obtain information from the Internet service provider for the site. In the government's thinking, this search was permissible under the act, because records maintained by Internet service providers can now be seized by self-written search warrants. Why is the government so anxious to by-pass constitutional safeguards? Answer: It's a lot easier to assemble evidence when the Constitution is not in your way.

In 2004, two Kentucky residents, Jane and Terry Adkins, allegedly possessed child pornography on their home computer. The government used provisions of the PATRIOT Act to obtain evidence against them. During the proceedings, even their defense attorney did not know that prosecutors had obtained evidence via the PATRIOT Act. The fact that the act had been implicated was only discovered when the Justice Department published a report about its use of the act after the conviction.

One of the more insidious aspects of the use of the PATRIOT Act is the ignorance of the target. When the FBI came calling over 120,000 times, serving self-written search warrants on bankers, lawyers, physicians, pharmacists, hoteliers, accountants, Internet providers, and postal workers—all as custodians of the records and documents of others—none was permitted by law to reveal their receipt of the warrant. So very few of the 120,000 Americans whose personal records were seized know about it.

Obviously, notwithstanding the promises of former Attorney General Ashcroft, the PATRIOT Act is not limited to terrorism crimes. The *New York Times* has reported that the act is frequently used to catch drug traffickers. It appears that the act has been used hundreds of times in cases involving crimes utterly unrelated to terrorism.

CARDIAC ARREST?

As a professor at the University of Buffalo, Steve Kurtz used biological equipment and bacteria cultures as part of his job. In May 2004, his wife had a heart attack and he called an ambulance. When the police arrived with the ambulance, they noticed his equipment and became suspicious.

The police alerted the FBI and its Joint Terrorism Task Force. The FBI responded by seizing dozens of books, computers, and other equipment without a warrant from a judge. The house was condemned until the bacteria could be analyzed.

Professor Kurtz was accused of violations of laws expanded by the PATRIOT Act, mainly the U.S. Biological Weapons Anti-Terrorism Act. The grand jury failed to indict Professor Kurtz, but mail and wire fraud charges against him have not been dropped. This is another case of someone having his constitutional rights violated under the guise of the PATRIOT Act.

There have been cases in which the PATRIOT Act was used to target members of certain faiths, usually Islam. Brandon Mayfield is an American citizen who was born in Ohio. He married a Muslim woman and converted to her faith. As an attorney, Mayfield represented a variety of clients, one of whom was accused of terrorism. Mayfield had only worked for the accused terrorist on an unrelated family law case.

After a train in Spain was bombed in March 2004, Mayfield was arrested in Oregon, and was imprisoned for two weeks as a "material witness." The only evidence connecting him to the attack was a blurred fingerprint. Spanish authorities told the FBI that they believed the fingerprint did not match Mayfield's. All the charges against Mayfield were eventually dismissed by a federal judge.

Mayfield was targeted primarily because he was Muslim and had previosuly represented an accused terrorist. The FBI used a "sneak and peek" search warrant to invade Mayfield's house. This technique—authorized by the PATRIOT Act—permits federal judges to authorize federal agents to engage in home break-ins, without notfication to the homeowner. In the good old days, if the government wanted to examine your checkbook because it had evidence that you were cheating on your taxes, it would present that evidence to a federal judge and if the judge found that it was more likely than not that you were cheating, the judge would sign the search warrant.

Since the PATRIOT Act and its self-written search warrants, however, the feds now have two choices. If their evidence is too weak to induce a judge to find probable cause, or if they are just too lazy to prepare an application to a judge, they can simply write their own search warrant, serve it on your bank—which, under the PATRIOT Act, is prohibited from telling you about the warrant—and they will have access to your bank records.

On the other hand, if the feds really want to ruin your day, and they do have enough evidence of probable cause, they can get a sneak and peek warrant from a judge, break into your home when you are away, and take your checkbook. For six months, you'd never know that the burglars were the local friendly FBI. Before the PATRIOT Act let agents play cat burglar, they would politely arrive at your door, display the warrants, take your checkbook, and give you a receipt for it. Not any more.

WATCH OUT FOR THE MEDIA

Even journalists have been adversely affected by the PATRIOT Act. The FBI seized notes from several journalists who wrote about a computer hacker named Adrian Lamo. The FBI used the PATRIOT Act to get around the confidentiality privileges of the journalists.

The American Civil Liberties Union filed a lawsuit against the government in April 2004, claiming that the PATRIOT Act was unconstitutional. The ACLU cited the ability of the FBI to seize records from businesses without a search warrant and noted that PATRIOT Act provisions have been used to obtain information from Internet service providers regarding their users.

The Department of Justice was able to prevent the ACLU from making its lawsuit public for three weeks. The Justice Department cited the PATRIOT Act's secrecy provisions. Some sections of the lawsuit were eventually released.

In a case involving a library in Bridgeport, Connecticut, the federal government attempted to seize records without obtaining a search warrant. The library, with help from the ACLU, resisted turning user records over to the FBI.

Because of the secrecy provisions of the PATRIOT Act, this is virtually all the information about this case that has been made public. The exact identity of the institution, what information the FBI was seeking, and even the specific date of the instance are not known. The only thing we know is that the FBI is attempting to spy on citizens without following the procedures of the Fourth Amendment.

JOSE PADILLA IN CHAINS

Jose Padilla was born in Brooklyn, New York. He is a U.S. citizen of Puerto Rican ancestry. He was arrested at O'Hare Airport in Chicago for allegedly planning to construct a "dirty bomb." Padilla has a substantial criminal record, including jail time for shooting a motorist in Florida.

Padilla left the United States in 1998, and supposedly visited the Middle East and Afghanistan. He supposedly met with Al-Qaeda operatives in Pakistan and told them he wanted to learn to make an atomic bomb.

The government alleges that Padilla presented his plan to detonate a bomb somewhere in the United States to Al-Qaeda.

Padilla was not initially charged with any crime or given a trial. American citizens cannot be imprisoned without being charged with a crime. But President Bush classified Padilla as an "enemy combatant" (a throw away term that the government used in *Ex parte Quirin* in 1943 to try nonuniformed German spies as war criminals) and thereby got around this formality.

Padilla brought a lawsuit challenging his illegal detention. His case went to the Supreme Court. In June 2004, in a five to four decision, the Court held that Padilla's case was void for lack of jurisdiction. It appears that Padilla's attorney filed a *habeas corpus* petition in a New York court two days after Padilla was secretly and involuntarily moved from custody in New York to South Carolina. Because of this, the New York court had no jurisdiction to rule on the case.

If jurisdiction had been proper, a majority of the justices said that Padilla would have been able to challenge his detention. However, because of a technicality in where he was being unjustly detained, Padilla's case was thrown out.

In the case of Padilla, the government first accused him of the dirty bomb plot. Yet it ended by charging him on a completely different basis. Why? The reason is he was first taken into custody on information gotten from torture. Khalid Sheikh Mohammed named Padilla after being subjected to a controversial interrogation that included "waterboarding." Critics of the torture continue to espouse the idea that much false information is extracted by employing such techniques. Clearly, this proved true in the case of Khalid Sheikh Mohammed, and ruined Padilla as a consequence.

Thus, on the eve of the day its papers were due in the Supreme Court on Padilla's challenge to his illegal confinement, the government had him indicted on criminal charges in Miami and sought permission to bring him there. The judges of the Fourth Circuit Court of Appeals, before whom the government had argued that Padilla was too dangerous to speak to a lawyer, much less be in the general prison population, were furious and accused the Department of Justice of attempting to manipulate the court system. But the Supreme Court let the government proceed as it wished. The case of his illegal confinement is before the Supreme Court, where the Justice Department fears it will lose its case.

Others such as Yaser Hamdi, who is an American citizen born in Baton Rouge, Louisiana, have been detained in a manner similar to that used against Padilla. Hamdi was even imprisoned in the same military prison where Padilla was held.

Hamdi was captured in Afghanistan and taken to the United States when it was determined that he was an American citizen. He challenged his detention, as no formal criminal charges were brought against him. His case went to the Supreme Court.

In June 2004, the Court held in an eight to one decision that Hamdi was entitled to have the government file and prove charges against him. The Court also said that Hamdi was entitled to the assistance of counsel for his defense.

Regarding Hamdi's case, Justice Sandra Day O'Connor wrote that "a state of war is not a blank check for the President when it comes to the rights of the Nation's citizens." Rather than try him for a crime, the government summarily released Hamdi, just days after arguing that he was so dangerous to American national security that he could not be permitted even to speak to a lawyer and had to stay in solitary confinement.

Others weren't so lucky. Ali Saleh Kahlah al-Marri is a citizen of Qatar. He was arrested as a suspected terrorist while studying abroad in the United States. Al-Marri has been in custody since December 2001. He was indicted by a federal grand jury for lying to FBI agents about the dates he traveled in the United States and the dates he made certain telephone calls, and for possession of false credit cards. When he refused to cooperate with the Justice Department in its investigation of terrorism, as is his right, John Ashcroft asked a court to dismiss the indictment against him. The court did so. Ashcroft then asked President Bush to declare Al-Marri an enemy combatant, which he did, then whisked Al-Marri under cover of darkness from a federal holding facility in Chicago to a Navy brig in South Carolina.

Al-Marri could languish there for the rest of his life without ever having been convicted of a crime. He has no access to family, friends, or lawyers, and he may never see a judge, a jury, or a prosecutor. Under this administration's interpretation of the law, it's possible that he won't be charged, tried, or convicted, and all the while he'll be held in solitary confinement.

The president—using standards not legislated by Congress, not approved by any court, and not made known to the public—has claimed the right to incarcerate Americans as enemy combatants until the war on terrorism is over.

By labeling someone an "enemy combatant," the government claims it can take away a person's constitutional rights. The federal government will not allow an enemy combatant the right to an attorney, a speedy and public trial, or to confront the witnesses against him. As the cases of Padilla, Hamdi, and Al-Marri all show, the government is not afraid to use the weapon of classifying someone as an "enemy combatant" against both foreigners and American citizens.

In all three of these cases, the government relies for support on a misunderstood U.S. Supreme Court decision rendered in World War II. The *Quirin* case allowed President Roosevelt to arrest, charge, and try before a military tribunal eight German soldiers who made it to our shores. The eight were, the Court declared, enemy combatants because they had been uniformed soldiers of a foreign government on which the United States had declared war, and they were arrested out of uniform.

Nowhere in the *Quirin* opinion did the court say the president had blanket authority to declare anyone an enemy combatant at the request of the attorney general. Nowhere did the Court say the president could indefinitely lock up anyone who didn't cooperate with the Justice Department.

In fact, *Quirin* actually stands for the very opposite of that which the government claims: it says all persons in this country are entitled to basic due-process rights. The danger of the government's arguments in support of its policy of punishment by fiat cannot be overestimated.

The government wants to disregard—even avoid—the Constitution itself. It has told lower federal courts that the president is not required to reveal his reasons for designating a person an enemy combatant and that his actions in doing so are not reviewable in any court. If that were so, it would stand American constitutional law on its head.

The U.S. Supreme Court has held countless times that all persons confined by the government are presumed innocent until proven guilty, must be told the reasons for their confinement, and are entitled to challenge those reasons promptly in a court. And the Supreme Court has also held countless times that it has power to review and to void all acts of the Congress and the president.

For more than two hundred years, judicial review, by which the courts enforce the Constitution's guarantees against the wishes of overzealous prosecutors, has been the salvation of our freedoms.

The very core of American history, law, and culture condemns the ideas of punishment before trial, denial of due process, and secret government by fiat. But today an "enemy combatant" can be virtually anyone the president wants to pursue.

RAILROADING THE LACKAWANNA SIX

In July 2003, the U.S. Department of Justice held a celebration at which it handed out honors and praises to federal agents and lawyers involved in the prosecution of the Lackawanna Six.

It should have handed out indictments instead, because those prosecutors—or at least some of them—violated their oaths to uphold the Constitution in order to coerce six soccer-playing young men from Lackawanna, New York, with no criminal records, into accepting long jail terms, well out of proportion to their alleged crimes.

The six—all Arab Americans in their early twenties, five of whom were born here—were charged in federal court in the

Western District of New York with providing aid and support to a terrorist group before September 11, by attending camps in Afghanistan, learning about weapons, and listening to Muslim clerics preach hatred toward the United States.

They were charged with *listening* to others—including, in the case of one of them, Osama bin Laden himself—talk about causing America harm. The defendants maintained that once they arrived and met the people in the camps, they wanted nothing to do with it. But the government told a federal judge that since the clerics being heard by the six were preaching violence, the six had committed crimes of violence.

The court rejected that argument out of hand. After reviewing the evidence against the six, the judge wrote that these defendants—like all defendants—are guaranteed due process, and that federal courts should do more than just pay lip service to the guarantees of the Declaration of Independence and the Constitution; they should enforce them. "We must never adopt an 'end justifies the means' philosophy," the judge wrote, "by claiming that our Constitutional and democratic principles must be temporarily furloughed or put on hold in cases involving alleged terrorism in order to preserve our democracy. To do so would result in victory for the terrorists."

But within mere yards of where this fair judge sat when he wrote those words, the government lawyers who once swore to uphold the Constitution were plotting to put it on hold. According to a lawyer for one of the six—himself a former federal prosecutor—the government lawyers implicitly threatened the six during plea negotiations that if they did not plead guilty, if they did not speak up as the government wished, if they did not cooperate in their own prosecutions, or if they insisted on their due process rights, the government would declare them to be enemy combatants.

In that case, the so-called "defenders of the Constitution" threatened, the six would have no due process rights, no trial, no lawyers, no charges filed against them, and they would receive solitary confinement for life. There is no reported case in American history in which a court allowed a defendant to be told that his insistence on due process would result not in prosecution and conviction, but in punishment without trial.

It has always been the case that when entering a guilty plea—and when negotiating for that plea—the defendant's fears of punishment were limited to those which the law provides. Today, for the government to threaten that the punishment can be increased by fiat by the president after the crime has been committed is not only unconstitutional, it is tyrannical.

LIBERTY: VOID WHERE PROHIBITED

It is only a warped view of American history, culture, and law that could seriously suggest that constitutional rights are discretionary—that any president can strip a person of his due process rights. There is no Supreme Court case supporting or authorizing presidential enhancement of punishment, and the Justice Department knows that.

So, if it is constitutionally impossible for the government to strip a person of his due process rights, why did the lawyers for the Lackawanna Six let their clients plead guilty and accept six-to-nine-year jail terms? Because they knew that the government had suspended rights before and gotten away with it. They knew that the president had actually declared three people to be enemy combatants and kept them locked up without charges and away from their own lawyers. And before the Supreme Court stepped in, he appeared to be getting away with it.[1]

THE "NEW" PATRIOT ACT: IT KEEPS GETTING WORSE!

The compromise version of the PATRIOT Act to which House and Senate conferees at the time of this writing, and for which the House voted, is still an unforgivable assault on basic American values and core constitutional liberties. Unless amended in response to the courageous efforts of a few dozen senators from both parties, the new version will continue to give federal agents the power to write their own search warrants—the statute's newspeak terminology calls them "national security letters"—and serve them on a host of persons and entities that regularly gather and store sensitive, private information on virtually every American.

The new version of the PATRIOT Act, which the Senate was debating at press time, purports to make all of this congressional rejection of our history, our values, and our Constitution the law of the land.

Why would Congress, whose members swore to uphold the Constitution, authorize such a massive evasion of it by the federal agents we have come to rely upon to protect our freedoms?

Why would Congress nullify the Fourth Amendment guaranteed right to privacy for which our forebearers have fought and paid dearly? How could the men and women we elect to fortify our freedoms and write our laws so naïvely embrace the less-freedom-equals-more-security canard? Why have we fought for 230 years to keep foreign governments from eviscerating our freedoms if we will voluntarily let our own government do so?

The unfortunate answer to these questions is that those in government do not feel constrained by the Constitution. They think they can do whatever they want. They have hired vast teams of government lawyers to twist and torture the plain meaning of the

Fourth Amendment to justify their aggrandizement of power to themselves. Their only fear is being overruled by judges. And in the case of the PATRIOT Act, they should be afraid. The federal judges who have published opinions on the challenges to it have all found it constitutionally flawed.

The Fourth Amendment worked for two hundred years to facilitate law enforcement and protect constitutional freedoms before Congress began to cut holes in it. Judges sit in every state in the Union 24/7 to hear probable cause applications for search warrants. There is simply no real demonstrable evidence that our American-value-driven-constitutional-privacy-protection-system is in need of such a radical change.

A self-written search warrant, even one called a national security letter, is the ultimate constitutional farce. Why even bother with such a meaningless requirement? We might as well let the feds rummage through any office, basement, computer, or bedroom they choose. Who would trust government agents with this unfettered unreviewable power? The Founders did not. Why would government agents bother going to a judge with probable cause seeking a search warrant if they can simply write their own? Federal agents have written and executed self-written search warrants on over 120,000 unsuspecting Americans since October 2001.

Is this the society we want? Have we elected a government to spy on all of us? The Fourth Amendment is the linchpin of our personal privacy and individual dignity. Without its protections, we will become another East Germany. The Congress must recognize this before it is too late.[2]

TAP ON A WIRE

President Bush has admitted authorizing the National Security Agency to spy on Americans without first obtaining search warrants from federal judges. But his defense is legally erroneous, and it constitutes an assault on basic American values and core constitutional liberties.

The president's job is to support the Constitution and to enforce federal laws faithfully. In this case, he has done neither. When the government wishes to search or seize a tangible thing—or listen in on a conversation—the Fourth Amendment requires it to ask a court for a warrant.

This procedure reinforces the uniquely American value of putting a neutral judge between the government and its domestic targets. We have given the government a monopoly on the use of force. Like all monopolies, it requires restraint, and one instrument of restraint is the Fourth Amendment.

When President Nixon claimed in 1970 that he had the inherent power to wiretap antiwar protestors without search warrants for national security reasons, the Supreme Court rejected his argument unanimously. Indeed, the House Judiciary Committee determined that by directing or authorizing electronic surveillance without search warrants, Nixon disregarded the constitutional rights of American citizens; it voted an article of impeachment against him for doing so.

In reaction to Nixon's unlawful behavior, Congress wrote two new laws. One was FISA, discussed in chapter fifteen. This law made it easier to wiretap foreign persons by lowering the judicial threshold from probable cause of a crime to probable cause of "foreign agency." But FISA did not—and could not—change the constitutionally mandated standard for search warrants of Americans: probable cause of criminality. Congress also enacted a new antiwiretapping law. This made it a felony—punishable by five years in a federal prison for each offense—for anyone under color of law to authorize or install a wiretap on an American without a search warrant issued by a judge.

President Bush claims that Congress, in effect, repealed the anti-wiretapping statute for him when it authorized him to use force against those who facilitated the 9/11 attacks.

This is utter nonsense. A sitting Congress can repeal a law written by a previous one, but it is a given principle of law that it must do so specifically and directly in order for us to know what the law is. Never in American history has there been a repeal by implication, one with no reference to the statute allegedly repealed, one granted to one person under one set of circumstances. It is not likely to be upheld in any court.

The president has also claimed that he has the inherent power to abrogate long-standing criminal law in his capacity as commander in chief. When he claimed that he could lock up Americans in solitary confinement and throw away the key just by declaring them enemy combatants and that such declarations were immune from judicial review, the Supreme Court rejected his arguments by a vote of eight to one, and reminded him that he, like all Americans, is subject to the Constitution.

Why would a president who has sworn to uphold all parts of the Constitution and enforce all the federal laws authorize such direct violations of both? Why would he attempt to nullify the Fourth Amendment's guaranteed right of privacy on which so much public, legal, and social policy is based? President Bush does not recognize the constitutional limitations imposed on his office. His only concern is victory over "the enemy," whoever that may be.

In a famous Supreme Court dissent, Justice Louis Brandeis foresaw the articulation by a later generation of justices of the right to privacy. "The makers of our Constitution," he wrote, ". . . conferred, as against the government, the right to be let alone—the most comprehensive of rights and the right most valued by civilized men." The Fourth Amendment embodies this natural right. It is the linchpin not only of our personal privacy but also our individual dignity. No president and no Congress can violate it with impunity.[3]

17

CONCLUSION

Do we still have a Constitution? Let's take a final look.

We have seen from scores of examples throughout this book how all three branches of government have used official government power to twist and torture the ordinary meaning of the words in the Constitution so as to justify the federal usurpation of power from the states and from the people.

Do we still have a Constitution? In form, we do. The president is still elected by the Electoral College, the Congress still writes the laws, and the judiciary still interprets them. But the president issues popular edicts, like claiming the right to arrest Americans without charging them, and argues that his behavior is not even reviewable by the courts. And Congress allows federal agents to break into our homes and our computers and to write their own search warrants. And the courts have permitted Congress to regulate virtually every aspect of our lives under the absurd theory that at some imperceptible cosmic level it is all "interstate commerce."

My favorite American president, Thomas Jefferson, warned that absent a revolution, it is the inevitable nature of things for government's power to increase and for the liberty of the individual to decrease. Unfortunately, he was right.

Do we still have a Constitution? We have the power to build

our government anew. The states—remember them, they created the federal government—have the power to force Congress to hold a constitutional convention to clarify just a few words in the document, so as to keep the government in check. First, "We the People . . ." in the preamble should be made historically accurate so as to read, "We the States . . ." Second, Article VIII which grants Congress the power "To regulate Commerce among the several States," should be amended so as to read "To keep commerce regular . . . among the several States." Third, the Tenth Amendment should have reinserted back into it the word "expressly," so that it will read: "The powers not expressly delegated to the United States by the Constitution, nor prohibited by it to the States, are reserved to the States respectively, or to the people." Fourth, the Sixteenth Amendment, which authorizes Congress to tax personal incomes, should be abolished outright. It is the constant stream of money from this source that has corrupted every tax-and-spend Congress for the past ninety years. Fifth, the Seventeenth Amendment, which provides for the popular election of senators, should be abolished. This would return their election to state legislatures and thus would guarantee representation of the states as sovereign entities in the federal government. The more sovereign the states are, the more independent will be their laws thus ensuring more choices to Americans. Ronald Reagan loved this concept, and said it enabled us "to vote with our feet," by moving to a state whose laws we prefer. Choice equals freedom.

Finally, if any lesson is clear from this history, it is that the federal government will never check its own power. On the contrary, it will continue to take liberty and thus property whenever and from whomsoever it wishes. Thus, I would clarify the right of the states to secede from the Union, losing all the benefits that come from membership, but regaining all the freedom membership has taken away. This is not as drastic as it sounds. The United States has had territories and commonwealths for over one hundred years. Many enjoy great prosperity and quiescence without a federal boot on their throats. And their residents do not pay a federal income tax.

The Founders did not give us a perfect system of government, but they did give us one that they intended would keep power diffused between the states and the federal government and further diffused within the federal government itself. And they gave us a document that recognized that our rights are natural, that is, they come from our humanity, thus from our Creator, not from the government. Ronald Reagan reminded us many times that we have the power to begin the world anew. I agree—we should start with a government faithful to the Constitution, one whose mantra is freedom, not safety, one that acknowledges that the government is the servant, not the master.

The Constitution, as Justice Felix Frankfurter reminded his colleagues from time to time, was not written in order to right every wrong. It was not written to allow every federal do-gooder and busybody to impose his notion of clean living, safe working, or pure thinking on individuals. It was written to keep governmental power diffused, to restrain the government from interfering with the Natural Law, toward one solitary goal: the freedom of the individual to pursue happiness.

Do we still have a Constitution? Dear reader, you can make that call. I say it has been sent into exile, and we must reclaim it before it is too late.

ACKNOWLEDGMENTS

Whenever I have written anything, I am indebted to those who have helped me behind the scenes. This book is no different.

Thus I record my debt to my personal assistants, Cheryl Romeo, Ciara Sullivan, and Dana Micheli. They have labored over endless versions of this manuscript with skill and patience. I thank my researchers, Marina Bejarano and Asha Smith, for all their work. I thank Darren Russell, my principal researcher, who put this ex-constitutional law professor through the intellectual ringer and who steadfastly and faithfully verified all my arguments. Joel Miller, my editor at Thomas Nelson, Inc., was invaluable to me in producing this work; without his patience, persistence, and professionalism we would not have this book. I thank James Conley Sheil, who reviewed and challenged, patiently and tirelessly, all my arguments. Finally, I thank Roger Ailes, who has continued to provide me the forum from which to explain American law and to defend America's freedoms.

NOTES

INTRODUCTION

1. Charles Rice, "50 Questions on the Natural Law" (San Francisco: Ignatius Press, 1995), pp. 21-22, quoting Clarence Thomas, "The Higher Law Background of the Privileges or Immunities Clause of the Fourteenth Amendment," *12 Harv. J.L. & Pub. Policy 63, 63–64 (1989).*

   For those wishing to examine a solid, easy-to-read introduction to the Natural Law, Professor Rice has produced one here. This well-footnoted and highly regarded summary of the Natural Law will be valuable to beginners and those looking for a refresher course as well. Professor Rice's research into original sources is so extensive that even those well schooled in the Natural Law will find his footnotes and bibliography quite helpful.
2. Rice, "50 Questions on the Natural Law," pp. 27–28.
3. Thomas Paine's *Rights of Man*, http://www.ushistory.org/ paine/rights/.

   A longer excerpt from this classic work reads, "Natural rights are those which appertain to man in right of his existence. Of this kind are all the intellectual rights, or rights of the mind, and also all those rights of acting as an individual for his own comfort and happiness, which are not injurious to the natural rights of others. Civil rights are those, which appertain to man in right of his being a member of society. Every civil right has for its foundation some natural right pre-existing in the individual, but to the enjoyment of which his individual power is not, in all cases, sufficiently competent."
4. Thomas Jefferson, "A Summary View of the Rights of British America," B.1.135. libertyonline.hypermall.com/Jefferson/ Summaryview.html.

   Given these and other references to God in Jefferson's writings, it should be noted that his position on Natural Law was not a function of religion or religiosity, nor are these references clear endorsements of Christianity. While he acknowledged a Supreme Being eloquently and frequently, Jefferson did not seem to believe in the God of Christianity. Though he quoted Him often, he rejected the idea of Christ's divinity.
5. Rice, "50 Questions on the Natural Law," p. 28.

NOTES

CHAPTER 1

1. Prior to the American Revolution, the British passed the Quartering Act. Under this act, the colonists were forced to provide housing, bedding, and even beverages to British soldiers in the colonies. Enforcement of this act was widespread and hated.
2. See http://supreme.lp.findlaw.com/documents/consthist. html.

   Findlaw.com has a plethora of the actual texts of Supreme Court decisions. Given that the Constitution is not a document intended for lawyers to twist and distort, but rather for every American citizen to read, interpret, and easily understand, I would strongly encourage lawyers and laymen alike to read the landmark decisions.
3. Thomas Colby, "Revitalizing the Forgotten Uniformity Constraint on the Commerce Power," 91 *Virginia Law Review* 249 (2005).
4. See *Federalist* No. 48, http://www.findlaw.com.

   The Federalist papers were written by the Framers as they developed, expanded, debated, and philosophized about the principles embodied in the Declaration of Independence and Constitution of the United States. They are a vast resource for understanding, interpreting, and realizing the plain meaning of the Constitution. Written in 1787 and 1788 with the intent of persuading Americans to have their respective states ratify the Constitution, the works were of a persuasive nature. Some even refer to these papers as the greatest public relations campaign ever staged. Talk about "Spin"!
5. See The Constitutional Rights Foundation at http://www. crf-usa.org/lessons/slavery_const.htm for more on this issue.
6. "The Rights Retained by the People: The History and Meaning of the Ninth Amendment," Volume 2, by Randy E. Barnett, George Mason University Press (1993).

   See this great scholarly work for a full discussion on the Ninth Amendment. The author has written volumes on this forgotten but important Amendment.

CHAPTER 2

1. By using the terms "liberal Democrat" and "conservative Republican," I by no means mean to suggest that the modern-day Democrats are indeed liberals or the modern-day Republicans are indeed conservatives. Unfortunately, both parties have so strayed from their philosophical moorings that it is often difficult to ascertain who is what anymore. Each wants more government and more power when each is in control of the government. Where have you gone, Barry Goldwater?

CHAPTER 3

1. Ironically, by today's standards, these small government Anti-Federalists also called themselves—of all names—the "Democratic Republican Party." How the times (and meaning of names) have changed!
2. The standards for toilets and urinals are articulated in "gallons per flush." The maximum for toilets manufactured after 1994 is 1.6 gallons per flush.

3. http://www.ag.arizona.edu/AZWATER/research/toilet/toilet. html.
4. Note that this is not limited to materials protected by the First Amendment. Section 215 also permits FBI access to medical records and other "tangible things." However, access to materials protected under the First Amendment seems particularly troubling.
5. http://archives.cnn.com/2000/US/03/31/census.01/.
6. "High Definition Interference," *Chicago Tribune*, May 23, 2005; See also "Court Yanks Down FCC Broadcast Flag, CNET, May 6, 2005, at http://news.com.com/2100-1030_3-5697719.html.
7. Nick Anderson, "The Nation: Republicans Indulging in Pork Along with Power," *Los Angeles Times*, December 8, 2003, p. A1.

CHAPTER 4

1. Thomas J. DiLorenzo, "The Great Centralizer: Abraham Lincoln and the War between the States," *The Independent Review*, Fall 1998, Vol. 3, Num. 2, p. 263, citing James G. Randall and David Donald, *The Civil War and Reconstruction* (Boston: D.C. Heath, 1966), p. 344.
2. DiLorenzo, "The Great Centralizer," p. 256, citing Robert Johannsen, *Lincoln, the South, and Slavery: The Political Dimension* (Baton Rouge: Louisiana State University Press, 1991), p. 81.
3. DiLorenzo, "The Great Centralizer," p. 256, citing Johannsen, p. 81.
4. DiLorenzo, "The Great Centralizer," p. 256, citing Johannsen, p. 92.
5. Thomas J. DiLorenzo, *The Real Lincoln: A New Look at Abraham Lincoln, His Agenda, and an Unnecessary War* (Roseville, CA: Prima Lifestyles, 2002), p. i.

   DiLorenzo dispels the myths about "Honest Abe" in this truthful and brutal work about Lincoln. He talks about Lincoln's utter disregard for the Constitution; his suspension of *habeas corpus*; his jailing of an opposing U.S. congressman; his true agenda of engaging us in a Civil War in order to advance a political view of centralized, strong, big government. DiLorezeno explains how Lincoln had several options to avoid the Civil War but exercised none of them. He simply could have let the states succeed, as was their constitutional right; eventually, they would have deemed it advantageous to come back to the Union. He also could have compensated slave owners and ended slavery, as did many other countries at that time in history. Every school child should be required to read this account of "Honest Abe."
6. DiLorenzo, *The Real Lincoln*, p. 267
7. DiLorenzo, "The Great Centralizer," p. 261, citing Merrill D. Peterson, *Thomas Jefferson and the New Nation: A Biography* (New York: Macmillan, 1970).
8. DiLorenzo, "The Great Centralizer," p. 261, citing Peterson.
9. DiLorenzo, "The Great Centralizer," p. 253, citing Robert Fogel and Stanley Engerman, *Time on the Cross: The Economics of American Negro Slavery* (New York: Norton, 1974), pp. 33–34.
10. DiLorenzo, *The Real Lincoln*, p. 258.

11. DiLorenzo, "The Great Centralizer," p. 258, citing Roy Basler, ed., *Abraham Lincoln: His Speeches and Writings* (New York: Da Capo, 1946), p. 583.
12. Thomas J. DiLorenzo, "Lincoln's Second American Revolution," on http://www.lewrockwell.com, November 23, 2002, quoting James G. Randall, *Constitutional Problems under Lincoln* (Urbana: University of Illinois Press, 1951).
13. DiLorenzo, *The Real Lincoln,* p. 272.
14. Thomas J. DiLorenzo, "Lincoln's Second American Revolution," on http://www.lewrockwell.com, quoting James G. Randall, *Constitutional Problems under Lincoln* (Urbana: University of Illinois Press, 1951).
15. Thomas J. DiLorenzo, "The Great Centralizer," p. 263, citing David Donald, *The Civil War and Reconstruction* (Boston: D.C. Heath, 1966), p. 79.
16. DiLorenzo, "The Great Centralizer," p. 263, citing Bart Talbert, *Maryland: The South's First Casualty* (Berryville, VA: Rockbridge, 1995).
17. DiLorenzo, "The Great Centralizer," p. 263.
18. DiLorenzo, *The Real Lincoln,* p. 137.
19. Lew Rockwell's essay, "Ex Parte Merryman and Abraham Lincoln's Suspension of Habeas Corpus."

    Interestingly, the government used precisely this argument to support its detention of Jose Padilla as an enemy combatant. ". . . the district court erred in holding that the President lacks the inherent authority as Commander in Chief to detain Padilla as an enemy combatant. . . . Neither the Constitution nor any act of Congress renders the Commander in Chief so enfeebled *when the enemy seeks to bring the battle to our soil*" (emphasis added). *Padilla v. Hanft,* Opening Brief for the Appellant, p. 20. This suggests that the commander in chief may be so enfeebled at other times, but his authority changes with the gravity of the situation that he faces.
20. DiLorenzo, "The Great Centralizer," p. 266, citing Michael Fellman, *Citizen Sherman* (Lawrence: University Press of Kansas, 1995), p. 141.
21. DiLorenzo, "The Great Centralizer," p. 266, citing Fellman, p. 145.
22. DiLorenzo, "The Great Centralizer," p. 266, citing Fellman, p. 184.
23. DiLorenzo, *The Real Lincoln,* p. 281.
24. DiLorenzo, "The Great Centralizer," p. 247, citing Roy Basler, ed., p. 652.

CHAPTER 5

1. I say "if at all" because the Natural Law tradition that the Constitution embraces has always emphasized consent as the essence of trade and as a natural right. The free market is created by the freely given consent of producers, workers, and consumers. To the extent that any government, federal or state, regulates the market—no matter how beneficial that regulation—it impairs consent.
2. Peter A. Lauricella, "The Real 'Contract With America': The Original Intent of the Tenth Amendment and the Commerce Clause," 60 *Albany Law Review,* 1997.

CHAPTER 6

1. This is my favorite line from all the Supreme Court opinions.

CHAPTER 8

1. See *United States v. Darby,* argued in 1941. *Darby* was *Wickard's* predecessor.
2. Stephen M. Maple, "Collection of Essays Revisits FDR Years," *The Indiana Lawyer,* August 7, 1996, p. 21.
3. Rexford G. Tugwell "A Center Report: Rewriting the Constitution," *Center Magazine,* March 1968, pp. 18–20.

CHAPTER 9

1. Fireside Chat on Reorganization of the Judiciary, March 9, 1937, available at: http://www.hpol.org/fdr/chat/.

   FDR's "Fireside Chats" were a key way in which he strung along Americans into buying his Big Government solutions to the nation's plight. These chats are legendary.

CHAPTER 10

1. See Richard Epstein, "The Proper Scope of the Commerce Power," 73 *Virginia Law Review,* p. 1387.

   Richard Epstein is a leading constitutional scholar, notably on property rights. His work has inspired and led the original "Constitution in Exile" movement. Justice Thomas's originalist judicial philosophy has been in sync with the movement's message of limited government. During Justice Thomas's confirmation hearings, the always laughable Senator Biden picked up "Takings: Private Property and the Power of Eminent Domain" and grilled the nominee about whether or not he agreed with such "extremism," who later gracefully crafted a political answer, at the hearing, but in *United States v. Lopez,* he wrote a sizzling, separate opinion, which affirmed the values of Epstein and other limited government leaders.
2. See e.g., *United States v. Darby,* 312 U.S. 100 (1941).
3. For more, see http://thomas.loc.gov.

   "In the spirit of Thomas Jefferson, legislative information from the Library of Congress" is the slogan of this vast resource for the concerned citizen or scholar of legislative activity. Aside from watching C-Span, this site offers a record of what your representatives are doing with your tax money in D.C.

CHAPTER 11

1. See *Gonzales v. Raich,* 03-1454 U.S. (2005).

CHAPTER 12

1. Jeffrey T. Renz, "What Spending Clause? (Or the President's Paramour): An Examination of the Views of Hamilton, Madison, and Story on Article I, Section 8, Clause 1 of the United States Constitution," 33 *J. Marshall Law Review* 81, citing *The Political Writings of John Dickinson 1764-1774.*

Dickinson represented Pennsylvania in the Continental Congress. He took his view of the taxation/general welfare issue to the Continental Congress. Renz has done an excellent job of telling the story and analyzing the great debates of Hamilton and Madison. Anyone wishing for an in-depth legal analysis of the General Welfare Clause and its true meaning should not miss this article.

2. Ibid.
3. For more, see "Debates in the Federal Convention of 1787 by James Madison," http://www.constitution.org/dfc/dfc-1787.txt.
4. Agricultural Adjustment Act of 1933, Section 9.

CHAPTER 13

1. Article I, Section 8, Clause 1.
2. *South Dakota v. Dole*, 483 U.S. 203 (2003) (Chief Justice Rehnquist writing for the majority).
3. Ibid.
4. See 10 U.S.C.A. Sections 654 and 558.

CHAPTER 14

1. Michael Kent Curtis, "Teaching Free Speech from an Incomplete Fossil Record," 34 *Akron Law Review*, p. 231.
2. James J. Martin, "The Framing of Tokyo Rose," *Reason*, February 1976.

   For a full examination of the terrible story of "Tokyo Rose," you must read this piece. Dr. Martin demonstrates the government's railroading of this innocent American citizen. The article details the corrupt trial and its biased judge, jury, and witnesses. Suitably, the article predates President Ford's pardoning of Mrs. D'Aquino.

CHAPTER 15

1. Sections adapted from Andrew P. Napolitano "The Patriot Act Just Got a Whole Lot Worse," TheDay.com, January 9, 2005.
2. Ibid.

CHAPTER 16

1. Adapted from Andrew P. Napolitano, "The Lackawanna Six Get Railroaded," *New Jersey Law Journal*, August 25, 2003.
2. Adapted from Andrew P. Napolitano, "How Congress Has Assaulted Our Freedoms in the Patriot Act," http://www. lewrockwell.com, December 16, 2005.
3. Adapted from Andrew P. Napolitano, "Constitutional Law: Walking on Thin Constitutional Ice," http://www. lewrockwell.com.

INDEX